D1447289

DEATH AND RELIGION
THE BASICS

Death and Religion: The Basics provides a thorough and accessible introduction to dying, death, grief, and conceptions of the afterlife in world religions.

It leads readers through considerations of how we understand meanings of death and after-death, and the theories and practices attached to these states of being, with recourse to various religious worldviews: Judaism, Islam, Christianity, Hinduism, Sikhism, Buddhism, Chinese Religions, and Native American belief systems. This inter-religious approach provides a rich, dynamic survey of varying and evolving cultural attitudes to death. Topics covered include:

- Religious perspectives of "the good death"
- Grief, bereavement, and mourning
- Stages and definitions of death
- Burial, cremation, and disposition
- Remembrance rituals
- Religious theories of the afterlife
- Death and technology

Featuring a glossary, suggestions for further reading in each chapter and key terms, this is the ideal text for students approaching the intersection of death and religion for the first time, and those in the fields of religious studies, thanatology, anthropology, philosophy, and sociology.

Candi K. Cann is an Associate Professor of Religion in the Honors College at Baylor University, USA. She chairs the Death,

Dying, and Beyond committee for the American Academy of Religion, is a former Fellow at the Center for the Study of World Religions at Harvard University, and a Fulbright Scholar at Han Nam University in South Korea (2023). Check out her website for a full list of her many publications, talks and interviews: www.candikcann.com

The Basics Series

The Basics is a highly successful series of accessible guidebooks which provide an overview of the fundamental principles of a subject area in a jargon-free and undaunting format.

Intended for students approaching a subject for the first time, the books both introduce the essentials of a subject and provide an ideal springboard for further study. With over 50 titles spanning subjects from artificial intelligence (AI) to women's studies, *The Basics* are an ideal starting point for students seeking to understand a subject area.

Each text comes with recommendations for further study and gradually introduces the complexities and nuances within a subject.

CLASSICAL MYTHOLOGY (SECOND EDITION)
Richard Martin

PLAY DIRECTING: THE BASICS
Damon Kiely

ARCHAEOLOGICAL THEORY
Robert Chapman

INFORMATION SCIENCE
Judith Pintar and David Hopping

DEATH AND RELIGION
Candi K. Cann

DIGITAL RELIGION
Heidi A. Campbell and Wendi Bellar

DRAMATURGY
Anne M. Hamilton and Walter Byongsok Chon

DEATH AND RELIGION

THE BASICS

Candi K. Cann

LONDON AND NEW YORK

Designed cover image: © Getty Images

First published 2023
by Routledge
4 Park Square, Milton Park, Abingdon, Oxon OX14 4RN

and by Routledge
605 Third Avenue, New York, NY 10158

*Routledge is an imprint of the Taylor & Francis Group,
an informa business*

British Library Cataloguing-in-Publication Data
A catalogue record for this book is available from the British Library

ISBN: 978-0-367-11129-8 (hbk)
ISBN: 978-0-367-11130-4 (pbk)
ISBN: 978-0-429-02507-5 (ebk)

DOI: 10.4324/9780429025075

Typeset in Bembo
by KnowledgeWorks Global Ltd.

For Maia
who taught me the "basics" of motherhood

CONTENTS

Preface: An Introduction to the Topic and Methodology   x

1 The Good Death   **1**

**2 The Process of Dying and the Definition
of Death**   **26**

3 Disposal   **40**

4 Grief, Bereavement, and Mourning   **70**

**5 Mourning and Bereavement from a Religious
Perspective**   **83**

**6 Afterlives and Afterdeaths: Remembrance
and Ritual**   **100**

7 Technological Afterlives   **126**

8 Conclusion   **143**

Glossary   148
Index   164

PREFACE
An Introduction to the Topic and Methodology

The study of death and dying, or as it is more clinically known, **thanatology**, is a fairly recent field of study and is taught in a wide variety of disciplines in college and university, ranging from sociology to medical humanities to religion, from psychology to anthropology to public health and medicine. The wide disciplinarity within the study of death makes thanatology a somewhat nebulous field of study with various disciplines claiming disciplinary authority over the subject matter, but each emphasizing a different (and equally important!) aspect of the field. Sociologists, for example, might examine death trends across a certain segment of society while psychologists might examine those same death trends from a perspective of individual motivation. A forensic anthropologist might examine the ways in which certain kinds of bodily decomposition reveal traumatic or unnatural death, while a biologist would examine that same decomposition from a completely different perspective. Public health analysts might examine particular trends in dying to critique inequitable healthcare systems, while a religion scholar might emphasize the religious worldviews of a patient and how this might impact **end-of-life decisions**. All of these different approaches to death and dying are equally important and reveal the importance of studying thanatology, but they all do so with different research methods and approaches. Which method and discipline speaks to you in the examination of thanatology may vary, but one thing is clear: The study of death, dying, and grief is important because not only will each one of us die, but also the way we approach and think about death impacts the way we live and the choices we make in life.

A BRIEF HISTORY OF THE STUDY OF DEATH

Because thanatology as an interdisciplinary discipline is still fairly young, and most people study death from a firmly entrenched disciplinary perspective, a brief understanding of the history of death studies as a discipline might be helpful for the reader embarking in this field for the first time. Thanatology did not emerge as a solid discipline until the 1950s, and even then it was not until Dame Cicely Saunders' founding of the hospice movement in the 1960s that death and dying became more normalized as a topic of study in the popular sphere (Saunders, 2001). Academics grappled with why death seemed to be a taboo field of study. English anthropologist Geoffrey Gorer (1955) argued that when sexuality became an acceptable topic of discussion, death became the "new taboo," while French medieval historian Phillippe Ariès (1982) wrote that death disappeared from everyday society, displaced from the home with the professionalization of medicine and the emergence of the funeral home. Tony Walter (1997) argued that it might have been the obsession with hygiene and sanitation that caused the movement of the cemetery from the city sphere to its outskirts. Whatever the reasons, the result of not thinking about death as a part of life meant that it was something to be feared or prevented, which in turn has affected perceptions of health, sickness, old age, and even science and its functions. As Fonseca and Testoni write,

At the apex of the crisis in our relationship with death, science began to be employed as a weapon in the battle against death. The concepts of health and death became dichotomous concepts, death being considered a sickness, as pathos. Within this context, growing old was correlated with physical malfunction and was equated with death (Elias, 2001; Kastenbaum, 1995; Morin, 2002). In recent times, this mentality has made it common to "treat" old age, for either health or esthetic reasons, as if abolishing old age would allow us to live forever, or at least to live within that illusion

(2012, p. 160).

Death and its study became contested ground as death and science became polarized from one another, as though science's whole purpose was to prevent, or even banish death. Equally problematic was the fact that many medical schools did not teach about death and dying, so that healthcare practitioners were little prepared for their encounters with death in the hospital.

Over the course of forty-five years of surveys from 1975 to 2020, sociologist George Dickinson (2011) has traced the expansion of teaching end-of-life care in American medical schools. He found that by 2007, while most medical schools taught at least one sixty-minute class, less than one-fifth of US medical and nursing schools offered a semester length course on death and dying. By 2020, this had not really changed. Interestingly, advances in technology may be inadvertently responsible for deceasing medical students' direct interaction with death. Dickinson's 2020 survey found that nearly two-thirds of today's medical school anatomy labs utilize virtual reality and 3D cadavers, rather than actual human cadavers (this is far less costly and allows students to easily practice various techniques on virtual bodies; human cadavers are expensive, but also prove far more interesting since each one is unique). Dickinson notes that as a result, medical students may be missing out on a key part of their medical formation. He argues that for most medical students, "Perceptions of medical students about cadaver dissections proved to be a crucial stage of self-reflection and useful for the formation of their identities as doctors, sometimes thought of as a "rite of passage" into the medical profession (Dickinson, 2022, p. 9; Yoo et al. 2021). For medical students preparing to enter healthcare professions, this presents a serious lack of preparation regarding death and dying, particularly for those who need to learn how to talk about it with future patients and their families. More importantly, within a medical care system that frames death as a failure, it has caused many healthcare professionals to feel as though they had not done their job well. It is important to learn that death is a part of life.

The emergence of the **Hospice movement** has also been key to death education, as it is a movement concerned with end-of-life and palliative care services, founded by Dame Cicely Saunders in 1967, at St. Christopher's in the United Kingdom. Scholar Robert Kastenbaum argues that the hospice movement can be viewed as a response to the impersonal, highly medicalized view of death, and its inclusion of an entire system of care (the patient, the patient's family, the community, and the medical practitioners) in its ethos allowed for a deeply transformational approach toward death that was more holistic than traditional medicine. Certainly, hospice care helped create more conversations about and around death, which allowed for death to become a bit less of a taboo topic. Similarly, Elisabeth Kübler-Ross's work on pediatric hospice, and her book *On Death and Dying* (1973) provided the first critique of a highly medicalized system of healthcare and publicly offered another way of thinking about both the dying process and death itself. Like Saunders and Kübler-Ross, Jessica Mitford's (1963) exposé on the American funeral industry and the death business, *The American Way of Death*, offered another important counter-critique not of dying, but of the funeral industry. Mitford examined the business practices of the funeral industry, exposing the predatory practices of the industry and the ways in which they took advantage of their grieving customers. Mitford's book eventually led to a second reprint and was fundamental to the establishment of government oversight of the funeral industry in the United States. Death studies has emerged largely as a critique and commentary to the totalizing influence of social constructs and beliefs surrounding the ways in which people live. To study death is to bring meaning to life.

WHY THIS BOOK?

Writing a book titled *Death and Religion: The Basics* is a fairly ambitious undertaking—particularly when there are many different religions, cultures, and even different definitions of what it means to die, or how each culture or religion believes we should grieve. Thus, this book is not meant to be comprehensive, but intends to be an introduction to the vastly wide intersection between both thanatology and religion. It is my hope that this book will aid the reader by offering a concise explanation of dying, death, and grief from an accessible and readable viewpoint that will inspire further research. This book will lead readers through considerations of how we understand meanings of death and after-death, whether in grief, afterlife conceptions, or technologies. Most importantly, this book questions the ways in which religion might impact the dying process, disposal practices, and mourning customs. It is important as our world becomes increasingly pluralistic and inter-religious that we have at least a rudimentary understanding of the ways in which different religious traditions and cultures understand death and the afterlife, as these cosmological conceptions often impact the way we view the world and how we view the role of grief and mourning in our cultures.

A FEW CAVEATS

With every book, there are difficult decisions about what must be written and what must be left out. As such, it should be noted that within each religious tradition itself there is often wide diversity that a book covering "The Basics" cannot possibly address, and the rich variety within each tradition is sometimes overlooked in favor of a general framework in order to inform the reader. Additionally, religious traditions have great historical and cultural diversity, but because these religions experience change and develop over time, many of the religious customs and traditions described here cannot be taken as normative in all times and places. Religion is dynamic and constantly changing, and I have chosen to focus on contemporary lived religion, rather than utilize the traditional historical approach. I have done this primarily because there are many books written from the historical and textual perspective, but there is not enough written about how people actually live out their religious beliefs and practices, and I feel that this perspective will be the most useful for those working in medical environments or with religious communities. I have always felt that religion is what people *do* and not what people say they believe. Regrettably there are also some gaps and silences in this text as I have mainly focused on larger religions with substantial numbers of adherents. For this reason, some religions have been left out, and while I wish I could include all religious customs and practices, it is my hope that this book inspires you to do further research on your own. On a last note, this text explicitly deals with death in parts of the world where Western medical technology is predominant and widely used and where people generally have access and resources to Western medicine. People in rural undeveloped areas with a lack of access to medical care will not have the same anxieties or options as the readers of this book.

BOOK STRUCTURE

For those newer to the field of thanatology, this book offers a comprehensive understanding of the field of death studies and the history of definitions of death (brain, cardio-pulmonary, etc.) and the relationship of these various definitions to religious understandings of the afterlife. It is my hope that this book will educate and prepare those planning to work with populations from a variety of multi-cultural and multi-religious backgrounds in the hospital or religious setting, so that they are better equipped to work with populations who may hold a differing viewpoint from their own.

The outline of the chapters in this book is below:

- Chapter 1: The Good Death
  This chapter examines death in a highly medicalized culture that tends toward death denial. An examination of the intersection of medical culture with various religious worldviews will be made. The chapter then examines the understanding of dying across religions and examines how "the good death" might be defined and understood in each religious tradition.
- Chapter 2: The Process of Dying and the Definition of Death
  This chapter examines definitions of death (cardio-pulmonary death, partial brain death, and whole brain death), the differences between these various types of death and why and how they matter, particularly in light of religious understanding and conceptions of the afterlife.
- Chapter 3: Disposal
  This chapter examines various forms of disposal, including burial, cremation, and other emergent technologies such as reef burial, burial pods, etc., studying the ways in which religions

prescribe or proscribe particular disposal traditions. In addition, the chapter examines the latest technologies in death disposal examining the ways in which technology impacts death and remembrance rituals across religions.

- Chapter 4: Grief, Bereavement, and Mourning
  This chapter addresses the role of grief, the development of grief theory, focusing on psychological and sociological theories on grief. It examines the ways in which these theories have either helped or hindered grieving, and provides a lens through which to examine the religious ritualization of grief and bereavement.

- Chapter 5: Mourning and Bereavement from a Religious Perspective
  This chapter turns toward various religious understandings and interpretations on grief, as a way to examine grief from both an academic and religious perspective, and also serves as a good intermediary chapter between death practices and religious grieving rituals, in which the various religious concepts of the afterlife are examined.

- Chapter 6: Afterlives and Afterdeaths: Remembrance and Ritual
  This chapter explores various conceptions and understandings of the afterlife in different religious traditions and how these conceptions have, in turn, shaped thoughts on death and dying, and the ways in which people interpret death after life. Focus here will be placed on examining religious notions of afterlife and how they intersect with death practices and the implications of afterlife belief on those practices.

- Chapter 7: Technological Afterlives
  This chapter examines the shifting landscape of grief and afterlife beliefs and how technology developments may influence that landscape. Particular attention will be paid to emergent technologies surrounding alternate afterlives through transhumanism, the Internet, smartphones, etc., examining the ways in which technology and death intersect.

- Chapter 8: Conclusion
  This chapter concludes the landscape of dying, death, grief, and the afterlife, with final reflections examining non-religious points of view.

Lastly, it is my hope that you will come away from this book not merely having learned more, but that you think about death in your life too. We all die. But that doesn't need to scare us. Death can prepare us and help us live better lives, full of rich meaning and joy. It can also help us live with more care and compassion for others. Death is a part of everyday life and it is important that we live life fully each and every day.

Questions about Death

Ask yourself some of these questions about death.

1. If you were to die today, is there anything you would regret not doing?
2. What can you learn from your inevitable death?
3. Have you shown those around you that you care for them if they were to die this week, next month, this year?
4. What do you think about the afterlife? Is it real? If so, what does it look like, sound like, smell like? If not, what do you think happens when you die?
5. What are you most proud of in your life?
6. What do you want your life to look like when you die?

REFERENCES

Ariès, Philippe. *The Hour of Our Death.* New York: Vintage, 1982.

Dickinson, George E. "End-of-Life Offerings in U.S. Medical Schools: 1975–2020." (Manuscript submitted for publication). Sociology, College of Charleston. 2022.

Dickinson, George E. "Thirty-five years of end-of-life issues in US medical schools." *American Journal of Hospice and Palliative Medicine®* 28, no. 6 (2011): 412–417.

Elias, N. *The Loneliness of the Dying* (E. Jephcott, Trans.). New York: Continuum, 2001. (Original work published 1982.)

Gorer, Geoffrey. The pornography of death. *Encounter* 5, no. 4 (1955): 49–52.

Kastenbaum, R. J. *Death, Society, and Human Experience* (5th ed.). Boston: Allyn & Bacon, 1995.

Kübler-Ross, Elisabeth. *On Death and Dying.* London: Routledge, 1973.

Mitford, Jessica. *The American Way of Death*. New York: Simon and Schuster, 1963.

Morin, E. *L'uomo e la morte* (A. Perri, & L. Pacelli, Trans.). Paris: Le Seuil, 2002. [Original work published 1951; original title, L'Homme et la Mort (Man and death)].

Fonseca, Luciana Mascarenhas, and Ines Testoni. "The emergence of thanatology and current practice in death education." *OMEGA-Journal of Death and Dying* 64, no. 2 (2012): 157–169.

Saunders, Cicely. "The evolution of palliative care." *Journal of the Royal Society of Medicine* 94, no. 9 (2001): 430–432.

Walter, T. Secularization. In C. M. Parkes, P. Laungani, & B. Young (Eds.), *Death and Bereavement Across Cultures* (pp. 166–187). New York: Routledge, 1997.

Yoo, Hyeijung, Dasom Kim, and Young-Mee Lee. "Adaptations in anatomy education during COVID-19." *Journal of Korean Medical Science* 36, no. 1 (2021).

FOR FURTHER READING

Cann, Candi K., and John Troyer. "Trans-Atlantic death methods: disciplinarity shared and challenged by a common language." *Mortality* 22, no. 2 (2017): 105–117.

This is an interesting comparison of two English speaking countries and their systems of death education, training, and academic study. The reader may be surprised how much the medical culture informs attitudes towards life and death.

Fonseca, Luciana Mascarenhas, and Ines Testoni. "The emergence of thanatology and current practice in death education." *OMEGA-Journal of Death and Dying* 64, no. 2 (2012): 157–169.

This is a succinct examination of the history of thanatology and death education up until the early 2000s.

Mitford, Jessica. *The American Way of Death*. New York: Simon and Schuster, 1963.

A classic read, this book remains pertinent and eye opening more than fifty years after its publication.

Walter, Tony. "The sociology of death." *Sociology Compass* 2, no. 1 (2008): 317–336.

Walter does a nice job examining various trends and themes in the study of death from a sociological perspective.

THE GOOD DEATH

INTRODUCTION

When we study death and dying in religion, **death** is often examined as a static subject, while the afterlife is seen as a religious construction. In reality, though, the understanding of life, death, and the afterlife, all intertwine with one's religious understanding of the world. Additionally, many people view death itself as a static category, when in fact, different countries and cultures have different definitions of death (see Chapter 2 for more on the many various medical and cultural definitions of death). For this reason, it is important not only to examine the different religious views on dying, death, and the afterlife, but how different religious worldviews intersect with medical culture. This means ultimately examining the medical system in each culture, since that will shape how dying is defined and understood. For example, in the United States, the medical system is shaped by its reliance on private medicine, so most often, people view dying as a "failure" of the medical system, and doctors are charged with extending life (and the medical system financially profits from that point of view). Conversely, in the United Kingdom, where the medical system is socialized, doctors often have conversations about death with patients, since it isn't feasible or financially beneficial to extend life at all costs. This is an example of two very different medical cultures, with quite similar religious worldviews and a shared language. This one example demonstrates that it is not enough to discuss religious worldviews when talking about dying, since the intersection of religious belief with medical culture is so central to how death and dying play out and are understood. This chapter examines

DOI: 10.4324/9780429025075-1

how the "**good death**" might be defined and understood in each religious tradition. Thus, in this chapter I examine the intersection of medical culture with various religious worldviews.

RELIGIOUS PERSPECTIVES OF THE GOOD DEATH

In the study of death and dying, thanatological scholars often refer to the "**good death**" as one that is foreseen, planned for, and generally expected by both the dying person and those around them (a person who dies of cancer would generally be an example of a good death). This at first may seem like an anomaly to one not used to thinking about death in a positive way. But the aspect of *goodness* is that this death is neither sudden nor unexpected. Since we all die, and death is universally experienced, most of us have both time and opportunity to plan to some extent what should happen after we die and how we would and would not like our remains disposed. However, many people still don't have **wills**, **advanced directives**, or **deathplans** (as if somehow they do not expect to die!), so for many, even the good death does not feel positive. Those who are aware they are dying, however, have at least a small measure of control over how they will spend their last days—whether it is getting their affairs and estates in order, saying their last goodbyes, or simply doing the things they always wanted to do, even if the act of dying itself is painful or difficult. Doctors, medical personnel, hospice workers, chaplains, and even family and friends can help aide in this process by ensuring that conversation surrounding dying, death, and disposal are held, and that those surrounding the dying person manage their own expectations. By outlining one's hopes and expectations surrounding the dying process, the dying patient can alleviate and manage anxieties, have input into the way they envision their death, and have some control over the way they wish to be remembered. This also helps the family and friends of the dying person, since they can act on their loved one's wishes rather than guessing what their loved one wanted. This is why it is so important to have not only a will (or a **trust**) but an advanced directive and a deathplan. The good death is not necessarily an easy one—but it is good because it is intentional, thoughtful, and as compassionate as it can be for the dying person and those that love them. Here, I'll turn to the notion of what the good death looks like in different religions and cultures around the world.

The Importance of Planning Ahead

While ALL the best made plans often go awry, having them is quite helpful for medical staff, family, friends, and most of all the dying patient herself. Then, at least, there is a blueprint for a best case scenario and this alleviates many of the anxieties that surround decision-making in a crisis situation. When my mom died of cancer, she had an advanced directive (also called a **living will**) that expressed her wishes to be removed from life support in the case that her life would only be extended through artificial means. When the doctors said that she would not live if she were removed from the respirator that kept her breathing, it was clear that it was time for my family to say goodbye. It was much easier to remove her from life support knowing that it was her wish and it saved my family from arguments over whether to continue to sustain her life. It didn't make her death easy, but she had made it as easy as she could for us by having a deathplan in place.

JUDAISM

A monotheistic religion originating in the Middle East and with about 15 million adherents throughout the world, **Judaism** is considered the tenth largest religion. Concerning dying, death, and mourning, Jewish belief claims that all humans are created in God's image and thus the body, whether sick, dying, or dead, must be treated with respect. This core belief is called *kevod ha-met* and is the guiding principal for all Jewish customs regarding burial and mourning. Jewish custom tends to be very matter-of-fact and down-to-earth in regards to dying and sickness, and death is viewed as another part of life. Illness is viewed as a part of the experience of being God's creation, but not something God can control (thus sickness is *not* viewed as a result of a person's choices or actions, as some tend to believe). Medicine and doctors, in general, are seen as essential to helping God restore healing to creation, and for this reason, while sickness is viewed as a natural part of living, medicine is viewed as helping to restore humans to their full potential. Euthanasia thus is neither permitted nor looked upon in a favorable light, as it is believed that God gave humans life and it is not their right to take that life away. In light of this, organ donation *is* permitted, if it is done to save a life, and many Jews consider the act of donating an organ to be a *mitzvah*, which can be loosely translated as a good deed or even a commandment.

Because historically there was little intermarriage with other faiths, Jewish morbidity is higher in diseases that are genetically inherited, and thus more Jews tend to die from metabolic diseases, autoimmune diseases (such as Tay-Sachs disease), certain inheritable cancers (particularly colon, ovarian, and breast cancer), and heart conditions. There is no universal agreement on the actual definition of death in Judaism—whether death is defined by cardiovascular death, brain death, or both. However, when a Jewish person dies, they are generally not left unattended, and friends and family sit with the corpse until it is taken to be prepared for burial. A person known as the **shomer**, or watcher, sits with the body reading Psalms and reciting prayers on behalf of the dead. Originally instilled to keep watch over the corpse to prevent theft or critters from having access to the body, the shomer now functions more ceremoniously. The shomer is so important that some synagogues even formally employ them and dispatch them to stay with the corpse from death until burial.

Judaism has several rituals regarding sickness and the deathbed, and it is believed that the final moments are very important for a person's soul and preparation for the afterlife. During the final moments of a Jewish person's life, it is customary that everyone remains in the room with the dying person to bring comfort to the dying. For this reason, no one can leave the room except someone who is physically ill or overcome with emotion to the point that it is upsetting to the dying. There are two more exceptions—the medical personnel and members of the Cohen, the priestly caste in Judaism. A Jew who is a descendent of the Cohen clan may not come within four cubits of a Jewish corpse or a Jewish grave—therefore, though they may grieve, they are said to become defiled and ritually impure if they come into close contact with the dying or the dead. Thus, a Jew who is a Cohen will often be outside the room of the dying or may visit the funeral home but not enter the building.

A prayer of confession, the **viduy**, is generally recited before death. Similar to the Catholic prayer of extreme unction, in that it is a prayer of contrition, the petitioner prays to God to forgive her sins so that she may face death calmly and peacefully.

Before praying the viduy, it is advised that Jews first ask forgiveness from those that they have wronged (Judaism expects one to ask forgiveness from those one has wronged before asking forgiveness from God for those sins against God). It is also advisable that others—particularly those who are crying—leave the room so that the petitioner praying viduy may pray on her own. Finally, before praying, the petitioner should purify herself by washing her hands three times before praying. Only then is the petitioner ready to pray the prayer of confession. The prayer seeks forgiveness from God and prepares the person for death, although in Jewish folklore sometimes a person is healed and lives for many years following the prayer of viduy. Following viduy, it is common to also recite the Psalms, particularly Psalms 121, 130, and 91.

In terms of the intersection between Judaism and healthcare, Jewish law advocates for the alleviation of suffering and thus palliative care serves an important function in the process of dying. There does seem to be some discrepancy over the extent to which Jewish law advocates for the utilization of life-support technologies, and some rabbis argue that life support should be utilized to its utmost capabilities, while other rabbis argue that life support should not be utilized in the instance that suffering is needlessly prolonged. Like Islam, neither euthanasia nor suicide is considered a good death under Jewish law, as euthanasia is considered the hastening of death and thus undermines the sanctity of life, while suicide does not honor the sanctity of life given by God. Thus, in Judaism, the good death is one that embraces and accepts the reality of a situation while allowing for the sanctity of life without undue or unnecessary suffering.

ISLAM

In **Islam**, the good death is one that ultimately comes under the purview of Allah, as he is in charge of death, not humankind, or even medicine. As the second largest religion in the world, with two dominant sects—**Sunni** and **Shi'a**—Islam claims nearly 25% of the world's adherents in 2020. Strictly monotheistic, Muslims believe in one god, Allah, and that Muhammad was his last and greatest prophet. In Islam, it is believed that only Allah can determine the how and why of a person's death, and some (not all)

Muslims believe in **predestination**, or the belief that Allah has already determined what will happen to the deceased once they die. This belief can also help with coping skills regarding a terminal diagnosis. Death in most of the Muslim world is referred to as an "**Intiqal**" or a "transfer" to the afterlife. Muslims view death as a movement of the soul from one phase to another in preparation for the final judgment, and because life is viewed as a test for the rewards to be reaped in the afterlife, death is not seen as a negative end, but rather, an expected and natural outcome. Like the Hospice movement in the West, the ideal death is one in which a person preferably dies at home, surrounded by many loved ones. However, in many countries, dying at home is not feasible or possible, and in the case that a person dies in a hospital, medical personnel might find a resistance to sedation or the use of strong medicine that might dampen a patient's ability to perform their prayers. Ideally, a dying patient's bed should be positioned to face Mecca, so that all prayers, even for the unconscious dying patient, can at least fulfill that part of one's prayerful duty. It is believed that the dying person has the opportunity to ask for forgiveness for any transgressions they have committed in their lifetime, and it is common to read the Qur'an by the bedside of the dying person. Because a good life is one that has been lived well in submission to Allah, dying by suicide is considered to be a sin since it contradicts God's will. To die by suicide is viewed as a questioning of God's plan, and therefore is never considered to be a good death.

Contrary to medical culture, where the number of visitors is restricted, in Islam, it is customary for many visitors to come and visit the dying to pay their last respects and offer prayers on behalf of the dying person. In fact, visiting the sick and the dying is considered to be an important duty of a Muslim, so a dying person's friends and family are generally expected in this precarious time. Because of this, however, it is also believed that the dying days are an important part of one's life, and death should not be hastened. Doing so might prevent the dying patient to receive the full benefit of prayers said on her behalf or for a person to have a chance to clear any last issues or disagreements. Islamic teachings require the requesting of permission from inhabitants of a room before entering—even if it is a temporary room like a hospital room. This means that even (and especially!) medical personnel should expect to request permission to enter a hospital room from a Muslim patient if they want a certain level of compliance. In addition, some Muslim countries have separate wards in their hospitals for opposite genders (though rooms are always gender specific), and it is generally considered unacceptable to combine patients and their attendants. This is true even with medical personnel, and it is usually expected that male healthcare workers should not treat a female patient without another female nurse and a member of the patient's family in the room. Frequently, the extended social bonds and responsibilities of male members of the family to their female relatives mean that they are responsible for the security and safety of the well-being of female family members, and therefore it is better to err on the side of caution when treating members of the opposite sex. The good death in Islam, then, is one in which a Muslim recognizes that all things in life—even death—are prescribed and overseen by God, and that even in one's last days, one is able to adhere to one's prayer rituals and cultural customs, and have them respected by those who come in contact with the dying.

HINDUISM

In **Hinduism**, the notion of a good death is tied to one's belief in **karma** and **reincarnation**. Named after the Indus river valley in India, Hindus make up approximately 79% of India, and is the third largest religion after Christianity and Islam. Reincarnation, the belief that one is born, lives, dies, and is then reborn into another life, is dependent on one's karma, or accumulated good or bad deeds that one performs in one's lifetime. From the Hindu perspective, then, the concept of karma can be used both to explain and justify one's suffering, since what one does in one life affects the next. Additionally, how one dies becomes quite important since the way in which one dies can affect the outcome of the next life. The good death in Hinduism, then, is one in which a person is honestly and categorically facing one's deeds in life, atoning for poor choices that have hurt others, and accumulating good karma in one's last days through kindness, meditation, prayer, and a general focus on the divine. The good death should be one that is accepted and acknowledged without reservation and met with spiritual resignation. It is generally believed that if one has lived a good life, and accumulated good karma, then they will be born into a better life, and in this way death can be viewed as a step toward a better existence. Eventually, the goal of a Hindu is to escape this endless cycle of reincarnation and attain **moksha**, becoming one with the eternal divine and ending the cycle of **samsara** forever.

If a Hindu has not lived well, and has generated bad karma, then it is believed that they will be born into a worse life, but even in this circumstance, reincarnation then becomes an opportunity to do well the next time around. For obvious reasons, this means that suicides in Hinduism are never considered to be a good death, since they demonstrate that one's life was not well-lived. Suffering in dying, then, is either feared as a distraction from one's spiritual purpose or viewed as an opportunity to live one's karmic consequences in this life, while death itself is viewed more as a transition to the next life. In Hinduism, the spiritual goal is ultimately to be one with the divine and thus the various divinities are viewed as different faces of the one divine essence. Suffering in the end of life, of course, can impede one's focus on the divine, but similarly, taking pain medication is sometimes viewed as inadequately facing one's karma, so palliative care can sometimes be difficult in this situation, as medications are viewed as not only clouding one's mind and keeping one from the ultimate spiritual reality, but sometimes as an escape from one's earned and justified karmic suffering. One should not hurry one's death in order to avoid suffering, and because of this, sometimes medication is viewed in a negative light. In addition to religious reservations regarding the utilization of medication in the dying process, India has strict regulations regarding medications that ease pain, and there are laws that make it difficult for doctors to administer adequate medication to dying patients, if it is believed that these medications might hasten a patient's death. This results in more painful and difficult deaths.

Unfortunately, patients are not always aware of their own diagnosis, and there are multiple studies that reveal that families and doctors often choose not to include patients in their terminal diagnosis. From a non-Hindu perspective, this is often unimaginable and doctors will need to work hard to create an open line of communication with both families and their patients, in order to meet patient expectations and increase awareness. Gender differences also are important in palliative care, and female patients and their families will often prefer female medical care workers. The health-care system in India has a wide disparity in quality of treatment, with great variation between urban and rural healthcare, but gen-erally, private healthcare is responsible for the majority of costs, with nearly 75% of families bearing healthcare costs.

Like Islam, dying in Hinduism is considered a family affair and not simply experienced by the dying person alone. Family members often share decision-making with the physician and it is important for healthcare givers to include key family members in the health-care decisions and discussion, in order to best care for the patient. Many family members will visit the dying person in their end of life and visiting hours—or visiting policies—will frequently be ignored so that extended family and friends can pay their respects. Often family and friends will accompany the dying patient until they have been cremated, believing it is important for the patient to remain in community with their loved ones. If a patient dies at home, the pictures of the deities are usually turned to face the wall, and the body is sometimes placed in the home's doorway with the head facing south. This is because it is believed that the person will return to Mother Earth following one's death, aiding in one's reincarnation.

SIKHISM

Sikhism, with its 30 million adherents—most of whom currently reside in India's province, Punjab—was founded in the sixteenth century by Guru Nanak and is a monotheistic tradition that stresses the importance of kind and compassionate action. Sikhism is cur-rently the fifth largest religious tradition in the world and has approximately twice the number of adherents as Judaism. Guru Nanak was born in 1469 to a Hindu family and disappeared at the age of 30 for three days. When he returned, he began preaching the teachings of Sikhism and spent the rest of his life propagating Sikh teachings and traveling to spread the message. A good life in Sikhism centers on meditating on God and performing good actions and focuses on the three duties of **nam japna**, or keeping God in mind at all times**, kirt karna**, earning an honest living, and **vand chakna**, giving to charity and caring for others.

Those who practice Sikhism are almost always easily identifiable by what are known as the **Five Ks**, consisting of **kesh** (uncut hair), **kara** (a steel bracelet), a **kanga** (a wooden comb), **kaccha** (cotton underwear), and a **kirpan** (steel sword), which can be anywhere from a few inches to a few feet long. These five Ks are the outward identifier of a Sikh believer, but also contain a deeply metaphorical and spiritual meaning. Sikhs don't cut their hair because it is a part of God's creation, and keeping it uncut demonstrates one's submission to God. The bracelet symbolizes God's infinity, and the fact that God has no beginning or end; it is made of steel because it is not meant to be decorative or ornamental. The comb symbolizes the importance of caring for God's creation, and being a steward in keeping God's creation neat and tidy. The underwear is a pair of cotton breeches that does not come below the knee, and was particularly useful when it was common for Sikh warriors to ride horses. Finally, the kirpan, which can come in any style and is kept in a sheath and worn under or over clothing, symbolizes the Sikh's defense of goodness and the struggle against injustice.

In Sikhism, death is considered to be a natural and inevitable part of life, and when a person dies, it is only the physical body that dies while the soul lives on. For Sikhs, the ultimate purpose is to be reunited with **Waheguru** (Punjabi for "wonderful teacher"), as a drop of water might be reunited with a body of water. Like both Hindus and Buddhists, Sikhs believe in reincarnation, but the ultimate goal for a Sikh is to become one with God, and thus both life and death are viewed as opportunities in which one can reunite with God through liberation from the cycle of samsara or **mukti**. Because life is viewed as a gift from God, Sikhs do not generally advocate for euthanasia or suicide, because this is viewed as interfering with Waheguru's plan, and only God is in charge of the time, place, and how of death. That being said, Sikhs generally have no objection to organ donation since a large part of Sikh philosophy relies on the care and compassion of others. According to Sikhism, the most important aspect of a good death is that one has lived well and cared for others in their life. In fact, many believe that regular meditation on death will help the Sikh remember that this life is only a temporary one, and the purpose of life is to meditate on the divine wholeness of God, or Waheguru, so that one may break the endless cycle of birth, death, and rebirth and return to God. Being reunited with God is the ultimate function of both life and death—life through pious living and reflection on the one-ness of God—and death through reuniting with the eternal and leaving one's individual ego and attachments behind. The good death, then, is one that ultimately reunites one with the eternal.

BUDDHISM

At present, there are about 488 million Buddhists in the world today, and 99% of all Buddhists reside in the Asia-Pacific region. Half of the world's Buddhists reside in China, followed by Thailand, and then Japan. The fourth largest religion in the world, with 500 million followers, Buddhism covers much of Southeast and Northeast Asia, with followers from the **Theravada**, **Mahayana**, and **Vajrayana** schools of Buddhism. In all three branches of Buddhism, the belief in karma and its role in affecting one's rebirth plays a prominent role in thoughts surrounding both life and death in Buddhism, and one's ultimate goal is to achieve **nirvana**, the soteriological goal of being released from the endless cycle of **samsara**. The notion of the good death in Buddhism is founded in the example of the historical Buddha, **Siddhartha Gautama**, who is believed to have been meditating when he died, and there are many stories of monks and nuns in Buddhism who have emulated this way of dying.

Theravada Buddhism, originating in Northern India and found throughout Southeast Asia, centers its teachings on mode-ling oneself after the historical Buddha. This branch of Buddhism challenges traditional notions of religiosity based on belief, as its emphasis on practice and strict observation of precepts shift the focus of religiosity to "a way of life" utterly different from the Abrahamic traditions. For the Theravadin, self-enlightenment becomes the ultimate goal, centered around a strong monastic tradi-tion. **Mahayana Buddhism**, found throughout East Asia (China, Japan, Korea, and parts of Vietnam) makes Buddhism more acces-sible, allowing for intercessory enlightenment through the help of **bodhisattvas**, divine beings that delay their own enlightenment to help others. In Mahayana, it becomes possible to reach enlight-enment through prayer, recitation, and intercession, reducing the reliance of the lay person on the monastic community. **Vajrayana Buddhism**, found primarily in Tibet (and in Japanese Shingon), is a more esoteric school of Buddhism based on tantric teachings and heavily reliant on secret teachings passed from teacher to disciple.

In Buddhism, the core teachings follow the **Four Noble Truths** and the **Eightfold Path**, hinging on the notion of causing no harm to others, including oneself. This means that dying and death, like Hinduism, are seen as valuable parts of the journey of life and should not be hurried along in order to alleviate suffering. Essentially the Four Noble Truths seek to answer the question of suffering and why humans suffer. The Eightfold Path offers a prescription to suffering, laying out a path of actions one can take to minimize one's suffering during one's lifetime. From this point of view, the act of dying is viewed as a process, rather than, as is often in the medicalized West, a singular event. For a Buddhist, dying takes place in stages and must be done well in order to ensure a good rebirth. One's death, and the circumstances in which one dies, is simply another reflection of one's karma, rather than an endpoint. As Philip Kapleau (1989) writes, "Buddhism holds that because death is not the end, suffering does not cease thereupon, but continues until the karma that created the suffering has played itself out; thus, it is pointless to kill oneself—or aid another to do so—in order to escape" (p. 135). This means that both suicide and euthanasia—whether active or passive—are viewed in a negative light. To kill oneself means that one has not learned from their situation and violates the Buddhist proscription not to kill. The same can be said for euthanasia, which essentially hurries the process of dying along, rather than allowing oneself to learn from the process. That being said, however, while sometimes necessary to revitalize the body, life support can be viewed as unnecessarily prolonging one's death and suffering, and in this circumstance, it can be a compassionate act to remove someone from life support if it is merely prolonging the inevitable.

It is a little more difficult to discuss the intersection of medical care and Buddhism, since Buddhism is practiced in so many different cultures and countries. However, some generalizations can be made. China, Japan, Sri Lanka, and Thailand all offer universal healthcare that is affordable and generous, and Japanese citizens enjoy the longest life expectancy in the world. One of the most important aspects of Buddhist medical care is its emphasis on the whole body and holistic healing. Body and mind are not viewed as separate and the Abrahamic distinction between soul and body is non-existent. This means that mind and body are not only inter-connected, but in fact, inter-dependent. Additionally, the spiritual component of one's suffering as experienced in both body and mind is essential to one's well-being even in the dying process. Compassionate (medical) care that centers body, mind, and spirit as essential parts of palliative care is crucial. In fact, in Buddhist scriptures, there are analogies of the Buddha as a doctor, and the **dharma**, the Buddha's teachings, as a treatment for illness. A strong emphasis is made in Buddhist scriptures on the interrelationship of spiritual, mental, and physical well-being. The Buddhist view of the good death, then, is one that ultimately accepts death and fosters an ability to help the patient's family also accept the patient's death. The good death is another part of life. To be born is to one day die.

CHINESE RELIGION

The three religions of China—Buddhism, **Confucianism**, and **Daoism**—are traditionally known as the **San Jiao** (三教) or the three teachings, and it was common in China before 1949 to practice some aspect of all three religions in daily Chinese life. While Buddhism has been discussed above, Daoism is a nature-centered philosophy that teaches individuals to live in harmony with the world, while Confucianism focuses on ethics, morality, and social structures. Many people might have recited or read Daoist poetry, studied the Confucian classics to become a Chinese government official, and then visited the Buddhist temple to pray or attend a funeral. The average person did not hold strict boundaries when it came to the three religions, though one might have favored one religion more than another, depending on social status, geographic location, and social standing. For the purposes of this text, I have chosen to discuss Confucianism and Daoism together under the rubric of Chinese Religion and have situated Buddhism as its own category, since Buddhism is found in Japan, Korea, the Himalayas, and most of Southeast Asia, and is not exclusively found in China. Current Chinese Religion is a mix of folk beliefs, religious thought, and secular practices and the Chinese government has strict authority over which religions can and should practice in modern China today.

Mainland China has free public healthcare which is under the country's social insurance plan and covers approximately 90% of its population. The healthcare system provides basic coverage for the majority of the population, but, more recently, China has also seen a growing private healthcare sector. One is expected to pay for private healthcare services upfront and out of pocket, and one may be reimbursed for some of the costs or none at all. Chinese diasporic communities in other countries may have vastly different healthcare systems, and Chinese Americans currently represent the largest proportion of Asian Americans in the United States. Overall, end-of-life care for Chinese patients tends to center on a reduction of pain, not being a burden to family, being with family in one's last days, and maintaining one's dignity. The emphasis is not merely on the physical, but also the psychological and social aspects of dying. Chan and Epstein's three-year Hong Kong study of the "good death" among end-of-life patients published in 2012 found that there were essentially seven elements considered to be essential to the good death. These are as follows:

1 an awareness of dying;
2 maintenance of hope;
3 freedom from pain and suffering;
4 a sense of personal control;
5 maintenance of social connectedness;
6 preparation for departure, and
7 a sense of completion and of the timing of one's death (Chan and Epstein, 2012, p. 206).

One can see from this list that the emphasis on continuing one's life even while dying and affirming one's social place and connections is central to the notion of the good death. In addition, the family's well-being throughout the patient's dying process is crucial to the patient's feelings about their end-of-life. In this way, dying is not merely a process for the patient but for the entire family. Alleviating the family's concerns also reduces the patient's own anxieties about their dying. One of the more interesting outcomes of the Chan and Epstein study is their findings that those patients with more children (generally three or more), and those who died when they were older (more than 65), were positively correlated to have had a good death. This finding corresponds with the Chinese cultural emphasis placed on both long life and having large families, and it is interesting that in Chan and Epstein's three-year data-driven study, those that believed they had *lived well*, also *died well*. Thus, in China as in many other countries and cultures, a good life (or rather, one lived well according to the dominant cultural values) is a primary indicator for a good death.

CHRISTIAN PERSPECTIVES ON THE GOOD DEATH

Currently, **Christianity** is the largest religion in the world, with about one third of the earth's population claiming to be Christian. Christians live all across the globe, with one in every three Christians living in the Americas, one in every four in Africa, and one in every eight living in the Asian Pacific region, a marked contrast from the turn of the twentieth century when most Christians were found in Europe. Of those Christians, a little more than half of them are **Roman Catholic** (18% of the world's total population and 11% of the American population), one-third are **Protestant** (around 11% of the world's total population and 45% of the American population), and the remainder are **Orthodox** (4% of the world's total population with 0.5% residing in the United States. Most Orthodox Christians are found in Eastern Europe, and 100 million Orthodox Christians reside in Russia alone). Nearly two-thirds of all Americans identify as belonging to some form of the Christian faith.

Christians follow the teachings of **Jesus Christ**, a Jewish man believed to have lived on the earth over two thousand years ago, who spent his short thirty-three-year life doing good for others and challenging a society that didn't care for the vulnerable and the poor, before being crucified by the Roman authorities. Within Christianity's three main branches, there is a fairly wide variance between the core beliefs and practices of the Roman Catholic Church, Eastern Orthodoxy, and Protestant Christianity. Both Roman Catholic and Eastern Orthodox Christians practice sacramental Christianity, which is centered on the observance of Christian rites believed to have been ordained by Jesus Christ, and are considered an essential part of the Christian life. There are seven key sacraments, which include **Baptism** (an initiation ritual in which the believer is blessed by holy water), **Penance** (or a confession of one's misdeeds), the **Eucharist** (the eating of blessed bread and wine with the church community), **Confirmation** (Roman Catholic)/**Chrismation** (Orthodox) (a ceremony inducting a believer into the church when they come of age), **Marriage** (the joining together of two people in a relationship blessed and sanctioned by the church), **Holy Orders** (the appointing of a person to a clerical position in the church), and **Anointing of the Sick** (the blessing of a sick person with oil). Protestantism varies in both its acceptance and practice of the sacraments, though almost all observe the sacraments of baptism and marriage. In addition, Protestantism tends to heavily emphasize the importance of individual interpretation of scripture and teachings, preferring instead to rely on one's own understanding of God, rather than tradition and the church. To a non-Christian, this can seem sometimes confusing as it has led to a wide variance in what it means to be a Christian. Like many religions, all three branches of Christianity do not believe that suicide is a good death. However, there does seem to be an increasingly better understanding of mental health issues, and that suicide is not always a sign of a "bad death," but perhaps a sign of a life not supported well enough. Thus, while the Roman Catholic and most Protestant churches traditionally have not permitted deaths by suicide within sacred ground, this seems to be slowly changing. Conversely, the Eastern Orthodox Church still does not permit even a funeral service for those who have died by suicide.

American hospitals usually employ chaplains for both Roman Catholic and Protestant Christians (and larger ones in urban areas often have religious clergy on staff representing other faiths or denominations), who are available to meet with families and patients and help with ethical decisions that the hospital might face. The medical system in the United States is largely based on privatized medical care, and thus many of the decisions—both medical and religious—are usually left to the patient and their doctor to agree on together, based partly on whether or not the patient can afford to take on the costs of their medical care. Additionally, both medical care and pharmaceutical costs in the United States are largely driven by market forces, rather than the government (as is the case in most other countries in the world). This means that the United States medical care system is the most expensive in the world. Dying in the United States is not merely an existential issue, but also a concern fraught with worry over expenses. Hospitals maintain on-staff clergy to help their patients and families confront their worries and concerns, as well as maintain the in-house chapels.

Some Christians may incorporate the priest or pastor in the dying person's last moments, though the rituals themselves may follow more scripted expectations, and written prayers, particularly in denominations in which **Last Rites** or **Extreme Unction** are practiced. Usually, if the dying person is conscious, then the person will be given the rite of extreme unction or last rites, and asked to give a confession, and then she will be forgiven her sins by the priest/pastor so that she feels ready to meet her final judgment in God's presence. A major difference between Catholic and Protestant (particularly Evangelical) worldviews regarding the final judgment, however, must be underscored. For Evangelicals and many non-Catholic Protestants, death can present a particularly scary dilemma, as death brings with it a final judgment and a determination that one will either go to heaven or to hell (unlike Catholics who have a middle-ground in purgatory, and can rely on their loved ones to offer prayers on their behalf once they have died). Prayer and reliance on the scriptures are very important, as it is believed that a person should be ready to meet God and be ready for a final judgment. Baptist and evangelical Christians have no common book of prayer or formulaic rituals regarding the last moments of life, though generally if the person is still conscious in her last moments, the pastor may pray alone with her asking for forgiveness of her sins and address any last concerns or worries she may have so that she may die more at ease. Often the family will pray together with the pastor over the dying person, and prayers at this time generally shift from prayers asking for healing to prayers asking for God to accept the person into heaven. The pastor usually plays a fundamental role along with the family in the last moments while also providing comfort to both the dying patient and their loved ones in their last moments.

This next section addresses the notion of the good death in various cultural milieus—which while not religious traditions per se—

are in fact perspectives that have influenced the way life, death, and the afterlife are conceived and understood. Omitting them would be dismissive, but the reader should be aware that like the preceding religious section in this chapter, these observations are somewhat general, and do not take into account various cultural variations and interpretations. It is a fine line to offer a glimpse into a worldview while not mistaking that glimpse for the world itself.

AFRICAN AMERICAN PERSPECTIVES ON THE GOOD DEATH

Because of a long history of oppression and a mistrust of the medical system among the African American community (based on a very real and unfortunate bias found in medical care), many African Americans have long relied on folk healers in addition to medicine to aid in their care. Views of dying are generally holistic, with death seen as a natural part of life, and a strong reliance on faith communities and religious beliefs in end-of-life care. That being said, however, some prefer to keep their loved ones on life support for as long as physically possible, and as a community, organ donation is not very popular. Nearly 40% of all African Americans refuse organ donation, and do not consider it a top priority. In fact, among all ethnic groups in the United States, African Americans are the least likely to receive a kidney from a living donor. Additionally, the medical centers that have the highest treatment rate of African Americans also have the highest racial disparities of organ donation.

The larger family and extended community is often called upon and included in the last moments, as community is very important, and any death is considered not merely to be a loss of an individual, but a disruption in the general social fabric of a community. The community is often called upon or expected to care for the dying in small ways that might not be particularly expected or appreciated in other communities—for example family members might tend to the grooming and washing of the dying, not only as a sign of respect and love for the dying, but also as a sign that the dying are, in fact, still important to the community, while simultaneously preparing them to become an ancestor. Mary Adams Sullivan (1995) writes, "Since the physical self is not merely physical but manifests the spirit, attending to the body is a means of attending to the spirit. Having successfully assisted the spirit in its transition, the family can more easily reincorporate the deceased into the community as an ancestral member" (p. 164). Caring for someone while they are dying ensures that they will continue to be remembered after, when they die. Some view death as a freedom from all the suffering and pain in this life, so, in this way, death is sometimes viewed with a sort of joyful resignation that is not always found in other diasporic communities. In fact, the term most often used to describe this is "homegoing"; other frequently used phrases in describing death in the African American milieu are "passing over" or "crossing over," where death is viewed as the soul crossing from one form of existence into another. Often, death is not viewed as an end to a life, but rather a transition and a rite of passage for the soul to leave the material world and enter into the spiritual realm. It is an opportunity to become an ancestor to those who are living and the chance to return home to one's true spiritual home where one's family and ancestors now reside.

That being said, the recent Black Lives Matter movement has spotlighted the disproportionate numbers of Black Americans who die because of racial profiling and unjust policing, with more attention being paid to the significantly disproportionate violent deaths of Blacks in comparison to their white counterparts. Statistics reveal general racial disparities at all levels when examining death and dying. For example, from 2016 to 2018, the all-cause mortality rate among Black Americans was 24% higher than white Americans. Infant mortality rates reveal similar disparities, with African Americans having an infant mortality rate twice that of non-Hispanic whites. Thus, while one can understand the view of homegoing as being released from a life of suffering, it is important to note the ongoing tension of living in a country where one's racial identity results in inequities that cause one to die earlier and suffer more.

NATIVE AMERICAN/INDIGENOUS UNDERSTANDINGS OF THE GOOD DEATH

Throughout the world there are many groups of **Indigenous peoples**—the Aborigines in Australia, the Māori in New Zealand, or the Mapuche in Chile and Argentina—but for the sake of limiting the scope of this text, we will only be examining the United States. In the mainland United States alone, there are 562 different tribes of Indigenous peoples, in addition to the Hawai'ian Indigenous and Alaskan Inuit peoples. That being said, it is somewhat misleading to discuss an overarching "Native American" understanding of death and dying. Each people have their own set of beliefs, rituals, and practices surrounding dying, death, and disposal of the dead. That being said, many Indigenous peoples do believe in a form of the afterlife, and some understanding of a spirit as living on separately from the dead body itself, with a fair amount believing in reincarnation. Dying is generally believed to be a process, rather than a fixed point, and for this reason, many Indigenous peoples discourage autopsies, or medically invasive disposal practices (such as organ donation or embalmment), because it is believed that this disrupts the spirit's journey of leaving the world of the living after death. Though there seems to be wide variation between different Indigenous understandings of what happens after life, most view death itself as a natural part of life, and dying should be seen as holistic—incorporating spiritual aspects, and not merely physical ones.

Like African Americans, Indigenous peoples in the United States suffer from much higher rates of traumatic deaths than their white counterparts. Suicide rates are substantially higher, with both American Indian males and females having the highest rates of death by suicide, with 33% of all Indigenous male deaths and 11% of all Indigenous females dying by suicide (National Institute of Mental Health, https://www.nimh.nih.gov/health/statistics/suicide). Also, Walker (2019) writes that "American Indians and Alaskan natives have also been found to suffer from higher victimization rates of violent crime than White Americans and a strong majority of the entire Native population, 83%, have experienced stalking, sexual violence, psychological aggression by intimate partners, or physical violence by intimate partners (National Institute of Justice [NIJ] 2016). American Indians and Alaskan Natives were more than twice as likely to die due to homicide as other racial/ethnic groups in the U.S. in recent years (Indian Health Service [IHS] 2018)." This means that non-natural, traumatic deaths are the leading causes of death among Indigenous peoples, and that not only are these deaths incredibly traumatic, there is a silent epidemic that is not being discussed or addressed in American society, making traumatic death deeply problematic and overwhelming. Obviously, in this instance, and in that of the African American community, the notion of the "good death" is not applicable in the face of such high rates of death by suicide and murder.

In natural deaths, some tribes believe that burial releases the spirit from the body, and for this reason, disposal of the body must occur relatively quickly following the death. If possible, many Indigenous peoples will ask that a spiritual healer be present during their dying—to make sure that their spirit is ready and able to return to the spirit world. Also, many dying patients will want their families and clan members nearby. Sometimes, purification rituals, such as the burning of sage, tobacco, sweet grass, and cedar, will be performed to purify the dying person and prepare them for the next stage of their journey. Songs and healing rituals may be performed by the community around the dying person to help purify their mind and prepare them for the next stage. The "good death" here centers around the acceptance of the transition of the spirit from this life to the next, and whatever form life after death may take, and is almost always a death that is embedded in the local clan community. The emphasis on dying as a community event stands in contrast to Anglo-Protestant notions of autonomy and control over the dying process. The good death reinforces one's identity as Indigenous first and foremost—through a combination of sacred healing and an acceptance of one's impending death.

THE GOOD DEATH FOR NON-HUMAN AND ANIMAL DEATH

While the "good death" varies across cultures, it almost always includes an aspect of good living hidden within its definition. With animal death, however, a good death is not always similarly viewed. Sometimes a good death is a quick death or a humane death (such as prescribed by Kosher or Halal dietary laws, or outlined by the contemporary practice of euthanasia), but death among non-humans and animals does not always reflect the quality or even the quantity of life. Some religions such as Buddhism argue over the sentience of a living being to determine whether it is considered to be truly *living*, with a wide variety of interpretation arguing for sentience that is often more dependent on culture and geography (and availability of alternate food sources) to determine the sentience of non-human life. In other words, the very definition of living and dying is sometimes dependent on other variables that become justified and then codified through religious belief and practice.

Theravada Buddhists in southeast Asia, for example, interpret the Buddhist proscription against the taking of life as one that includes all living beings, sentient or not, while Japanese Buddhists view fish as remaining outside of this proscription. Tibetan Buddhists generally don't practice vegetarianism at all (largely because there is simply not the arable land available in other countries to sustain a plant-based diet), while Jains in India go to such extremes to preserve life that they consider the eating of root-based plants (like potatoes or onions) to be the taking of a life, since root based-plants do not bear fruit beyond the one vegetable.

Non-human death, and the understanding of a "good death" remains variable and dependent on the definition of what is considered to be *alive* in the first place. It is important to note here, though, that in much of the world, non-humans (and even young humans or children might fall into this category) do not have much, if any, agency over their lives and deaths. Most religions often categorize and hierarchize animal life in relation to human life, while offering only very minimal protections, if any, of life outside of humanity itself. The Abrahamic traditions offer a hierarchical schema of humans in relation to animals, with an emphasis on animals as serving humanity's needs and purposes, though there are a few traditions that emphasize the humane treatment of animals within this schema. There are also a few exceptions—such as the Seventh Day Adventists, who argue that Jesus was a pescatarian, and that Christian followers should follow a largely vegetarian diet and keep kosher dietary laws. In this way, the importance of the "good death" among non-humans is often minimized, if not neglected altogether, and the rationale for following many of these dietary restrictions are often not interpreted in light of an ethics for and about animals, but rather a healthier lifestyle choice for humans.

REFERENCES

Chan, Wallace CH, and I. Epstein. "Researching "good death" in a Hong Kong palliative care program: A clinical data-mining study." *OMEGA-Journal of Death and Dying* 64, no. 3 (2012): 203–222.

Kapleau, Philip. *The Wheel of Life and Death: A Practical and Spiritual Guide.* New York: Doubleday, 1989.

National Institute of Mental Health. "Suicide." https://www.nimh.nih.gov/health/statistics/suicide, last accessed May 12, 2022.

Sullivan, Martha Adams. "May the Circle Be Unbroken: The African American Experience of Death, Dying, and Spirituality." *A Cross-cultural Look at Death, Dying, and Religion*, Chicago, IL: Nelson-Hall Publishers, 1995.

Walker, Andrea C. "Death and Dying in American Indian Cultures." In *Death across Cultures*, pp. 335–349. New York: Springer, 2019.

FOR FURTHER READING

Muslim Perspectives on Death and Dying:

Sheikh, Aziz. "Death and dying—a Muslim perspective." *Journal of the Royal Society of Medicine* 91, no. 3 (1998): 138–140. https://www.ncbi.nlm.nih.gov/pmc/articles/PMC1296563/pdf/jrsocmed00027-0028.pdf

This article is written from the perspective of a British Muslim and was written to members of the medical field to offer advice in caring for Muslim patients with a fatal illness.

Hindu/Indian Perspectives on Death and Dying:

Sharma, Himanshu, Vankar Jagdish, Prabhakaran Anusha, and Sharma Bharti. "End-of-life care: Indian perspective." *Indian Journal of Psychiatry* 55, no. Suppl 2 (2013): S293. https://www.ncbi.nlm.nih.gov/pmc/articles/PMC3705699/

This article provides an Indian perspective on end of life care and is a phenomenal resource for the relationship between spirituality and medicine.

Buddhist Perspectives on Death and Dying:

Masel, Eva K., Sophie Schur, and Herbert H. Watzke. "Life is uncertain. Death is certain. Buddhism and palliative care." *Journal of Pain and Symptom Management* 44, no. 2 (2012): 307–312.

This article from the Journal of Pain and Symptom Management is a great resource for palliative care for members of the Buddhist spiritual and religious communities. 10/10 recommend.

Chinese Diaspora Perspectives on Death and Dying:

Lee, Mei Ching, Katherine A. Hinderer, and Carla S. Alexander. "What matters most at the end-of-life for Chinese Americans?." *Gerontology and Geriatric Medicine* 4 (2018): 2333721418778195. https://www.ncbi.nlm.nih.gov/pmc/articles/PMC6050625/

This article discusses the results from a study about Chinese Americans and their physical, psychosocial, and spiritual needs during the end of their lives.

Jewish Perspectives on Death and Dying:

Linzer, Rabbi Dov. "Treatment of terminally ill patients according to Jewish law." *AMA Journal of Ethics* 13, no. 12 (2013): 1081–1087.

This article presents ways in which the care of terminally Ill patients may be different according to the Jewish practices, customs, and laws. It appears to be a valuable resource for understanding the intersection of Jewish law with modern medical practice.

Schultz, Michael, Kassim Baddarni, and Gil Bar-Sela. "Reflections on palliative care from the Jewish and Islamic tradition." *Evidence-Based Complementary and Alternative Medicine* 2012 (2012). https://www.ncbi.nlm.nih.gov/pmc/articles/PMC3235784/

Another fantastic article found through NCBI. This article discusses palliative care for both Jewish and Islamic believers and the intersection between these two Abrahamic faiths.

African American Perspectives on Death and Dying:

Sullivan, Martha Adams. "May the Circle Be Unbroken: The African-American Experience of Death, Dying and Spirituality." In Joan K. Parry and Angela Shen Ryan, eds, *A Cross-Cultural Look at Death, Dying, and Religion*, Chicago, IL: Nelson-Hall, 1995.

This is a brief examination of the history of the African American experience of death and dying.

Cann, Candi K. *African American Deathways*. Oxford, England: Oxford University Press, 2020.

An exhaustive bibliography, this list walks the reader through the most significant publications on African American deathways, material culture, and current Black Lives Matter publications.

Indigenous Perspectives on Death and Dying:

Walker, Andrea C. "Death and Dying in American Indian Cultures." In *Death Across Cultures*, pp. 335–349. New York: Springer, 2019.

This is a great chapter in indigenous understandings of death and dying.

Meleen, Michele. "Native American Death Rituals." *Love To Know.* https://dying.lovetoknow.com/native-american-death-rituals *(accessed Aug. 13, 2018)* (2020).

Though a blog post, this is a helpful description of some of the major beliefs and practices surrounding death and grief in different Native American tribes.

Dennis, Mary Kate, and Karla T. Washington. "Just let me go": End-of-life planning among Ojibwe elders." *The Gerontologist* 58, no. 2 (2018): 300–307. https://academic.oup.com/gerontologist/article/58/2/300/2646632, last accessed December 2, 2021.

A case study centered on 20 tribal elders in the Great Lakes region, this article explains the importance of one's family and community in the dying process among indigenous peoples.

THE PROCESS OF DYING AND THE DEFINITION OF DEATH

THE PROCESS OF DYING

While death may be universally difficult to define, **dying** is the permanent and irreversible cessation of the biological function of life. All living organisms move toward death once they are born, but how one dies is generally not predictable. In Chapter 1, the various conceptions of the "good death" were addressed, and in thanatological terms, those who are able to know about and plan for their death (e.g., a cancer patient) are traditionally viewed as "**dying well**." Dying well usually describes a person whose death is somewhat manageable and under their control, describing a dying process that is somewhat predictable and offers time for the dying person to plan for and think about their death. Usually this also allows for the dying person to write a **will**, a legally binding government document that explains what to do with one's possessions and estate (if they don't already have one), complete an **advanced directive** or living will, which tells the hospital what care they do and do not want, and how far to extend that care, and to possibly even plan their funeral and/or final **disposition** (the dying person's wishes regarding the disposal of their body once they have died). In the study of death and dying, a person who utilizes hospice care in their dying days is said to be dying well because they have time to plan and prepare for their death. That being said, however, it should be noted that this examination of "dying well" can sometimes be understood and misapplied to impose a normative judgement regarding how one should die, or insist upon a set standard of expectations of the best way to die, which can be triggering

DOI: 10.4324/9780429025075-2

for those not matching expectations. It should be emphasized that while the term "dying well" is frequently used to describe some-one who has time to prepare for their death, there are many ways to die, and here the term is used in a non-normative way to describe an extended awareness regarding the dying process, rather than assuming a normative judgement of what that process involves.

From a clinical perspective, there are three notable stages in the dying process in someone who dies from old age or disease (obvi-ously this looks quite different in a violent or accidental death): the early, middle, and last stages of dying. In the **early stages of dying**, which lasts anywhere from a few days to a few weeks, there is a marked reduction in the intake of fluids and food. While family members and friends of the loved one who is dying will sometimes become distressed in noticing this stage, it is important to note that the reduction of both food and fluids helps reduce the suffering and pain experienced by the dying person as their body begins to shut down. By reducing food, bowel movements occur less frequently and thus cause less physical distress. Similarly, reduc-ing hydration lessens suffering as dehydration causes decreased swelling and a reduction in pulmonary secretions (thereby reduc-ing the need for the suctioning of fluids). Mild dehydration also increases the body's endorphins and creates a heightened state of well-being, decreases urinary output, and reduces fluid buildup around tumors, decreasing tumor pressure and pain, and lessen-ing cognitive function, which aids in pain reduction. In short, it is in the patient's best interests to remain under-hydrated during the dying process as it reduces pain, swelling, and fluid retention. However, many people are not aware of the importance of dehy-dration in making a patient comfortable as they die and will insist on artificial hydration.

The **middle stage of dying** usually lasts anywhere from a few hours to a few days, and in this stage, the dying person becomes increasingly unresponsive as the body's circulation begins to slow and the person's hands and feet become increasingly cold as a result. Putting socks on the dying person's feet and warming their body (particularly their extremities) and offering comfort during this stage is advised as a way to give the dying person comfort. They may move in and out of consciousness as their organs begin to fail. In this stage, the patient will gradually become less aware and may not be as communicative or responsive to those around them as their body begins to shut down.

In the **last stage of dying**, the stage sometimes described as **active dying**, the person's body begins to shut down completely, and either becomes incontinent or bowel movements may cease because of the cessation of kidney function and the relaxation of muscles. It may be helpful to ease the person's comfort with either a catheter and/or pads underneath the person. In addition, breathing becomes irregular and chest congestion can cause a "rattle" in one's breathing as the chest becomes unable to clear out fluids. Elevating the head can help with some discomfort in breathing, and the primary concern should be making these last few moments of the dying person's life as comfortable as possible through pain management and a reduction in consciousness, if appropriate. Those patients who are somewhat conscious in this stage will often experience delirium or hallucinations, and family members often describe their loved ones who are dying talking to, and with, people who have died before them. Some may find this comforting, while others may not, but it is very natural and normal as the person's body begins to shut down.

Also of note in this stage is the fact that many dying people might experience what is known as **terminal lucidity**, which is a brief and often unexpected return of lucidity and consciousness right before death—particularly in those suffering from neurological issues. Nahm et al (2012) found in their 2011 study "Terminal Lucidity: A Review and a Case Collection" in the *Archives of Gerontology and Geriatrics*, that 42% of those patients who experienced terminal lucidity died that same day, while 84% died within the same week. It is important that family and friends of the dying be aware of this phenomenon so that it is not misinterpreted as a "recovery" but acknowledged as one of the more common signs that death is, in fact, very near. Michael Nahm (the lead author of the above study) has done much research on the lucidity of patients who have been cognitively impaired for years—finding stories of even those with Alzheimer's and irreversible brain damage able to be clearly cognizant with their friends and family hours before their death. Understanding this phenomenon in this way may help friends and family to see this last rally as a gift rather than misunderstanding it as a sign of recovery.

HOSPICE AND PALLIATIVE CARE

There are different types of **palliative care** that aid in managing the dying process. Unfortunately, however, in industrialized society, death in hospitals continues to be the most common, with approximately 60% of all Americans and 52% of all Europeans dying in the hospital, rather than at home. Dying in the hospital is also the most expensive and invasive form of death, though there are other options that are becoming more widely known and utilized. There are two primary types of palliative care—hospital palliative care and hospice care, which can occur in a hospice facility or in a patient's home. **Hospital palliative care** is a hospital-appointed specialized palliative care team trained in managing the pain, symptoms, and stress of a patient with the specific directive of reducing pain rather than curing disease/illness. Palliative care differs slightly from hospice care in that it can be given alongside either **curative care** (treatments centered on ending or curing disease, rather than the management of pain or suffering) or hospice care, and is centered on creating the best quality of life for the patient. Palliative care is begun at any time in an illness, terminal or non-terminal, at the discretion of both the patient and the physician. In the hospital, if it is clear a patient is dying, the hospice care team and the attending physician will work together to determine what level of medical care is needed in proportion to comfort care.

Hospice care, however, is solely comfort care, centered on improving the quality of the end-of-life for both patients and their families. Hospice care usually occurs in a hospice facility center or in the home, easing the pain and suffering of a person facing a terminal illness with a prognosis of six months or less. For this reason, some patients and their families may be resistant to hospice care since it is specifically end-of-life care. **Hospice eligibility** in the American medical system requires that two separate physicians agree that the patient has six months or less to live if the disease were to progress naturally without medical interventions. Unfortunately, language utilized in the dying process—such as "fighting cancer" and "battling illness"—can negatively impact the perception of hospice as "giving up," rather than simply acknowledging the reality of a situation. Because of this, it is important to have conversations about hospice and to encourage people to rethink the language used to describe both illness and death as natural biological functions of the body.

Hospice care is holistic care that addresses not only symptom and pain management, but also mental and emotional distress, the support systems available to both the dying person and their family, and follow-up care for the family after the patient's death. Hospice care can be administered in the home or in institutional hospice care facilities. One advantage of institutional hospice care facilities is that people can receive around-the-clock comfort care in spaces designed for end-of-life care (e.g., the room can accommodate large adjustable hospital beds with rails and bathrooms have special accommodations for those in need of mobility aids) while not over-burdening their loved ones. Wherever a person chooses to die, however, hospice care includes a team of caregivers usually consisting of a physician, nurses, chaplains, social workers, and volunteers so that both the dying person and their loved ones never feel alone.

Living Wills and Advanced Directives

Do you have a Living Will or an Advanced Directive? These are important documents that can serve as your proxy in the case that you are incapacitated and receiving medical care. They are legally binding and can also help your family decide how to best care for you in case you can no longer communicate your wishes to them. You can designate another family member or loved one to make decisions for you, and you can outline what kind of care you do and do not want. You should include things like: What kind of medical interventions do you want should you become incapacitated? Should you be permanently incapacitated, what kinds of medical interventions do you want? Do you want to be resuscitated? What kind of pain management do you want? Do you want to donate your organs? If so, which ones? These are only a few of the questions that should be answered in your living will, but having one will greatly reduce any anxieties that you and your loved ones might have regarding the outcome of your care.

DEFINING DEATH

Now that we have studied the dying process and the various types of end-of-life care available in this final stage, it is important to examine more in depth the actual definition of death itself. The differences between cardio-pulmonary death, partial brain death, and whole brain death are important and different countries and medical systems employ these different definitions to determine that a person has died. As the study of the definition of a good death reveals, the cultural, geographical, and temporal context of death all matter. And as technology has advanced and countries have become wealthier and more able to afford expensive and innovative medical equipment, the dying process has become extended and people have been able to live far longer lives, pushing the definitions of dying and death to new boundaries. Medical innovation and technological expansion have also, however, blurred the boundaries between life and death, allowing people to die and be resuscitated, to live longer because of organ donation, and to create new definitions of death that are a direct result of medical technology. It is difficult to acknowledge death when parts of the body (the brain or the heart) are intentionally kept living in order to facilitate **organ transplant**, or because of one's religious convictions. Death in the contemporary world has become less clear-cut and more confusing—even at the biological level—but certainly at an ethical one. The question today is not so much whether a person is dead, but whether they are "dead enough" to be considered to be no longer living. Even after a body has been declared dead, dead bodies in hospitals are often considered to be a sum of body parts (in that a person might donate their eyes, for example, or one's lungs, or even one's entire corpse to be studied after death in a medical student's anatomy lab), so that death seems to occur in pieces or in steps, rather than all at once. Does this aid the dying process or make it more confusing and difficult?

CARDIO-PULMONARY DEATH

Today, there are three primary definitions of death that are globally dominant. These are cardio-pulmonary death, whole brain death, and partial brain death. **Cardio-pulmonary death** is when the heart and lungs cease to function, blood no longer flows, the heart stops pumping, and lungs no longer circulate air through the circulatory system. Cardio-pulmonary death is considered the traditional definition of death and was the primary understanding of death until the twentieth century and the 1950s and 1960s when organ transplant surgery first began and the practice of cardio-pulmonary resuscitation (CPR) first emerged. CPR's emergence in the 1960s created a new understanding of cardio-pulmonary issues, since death could now be reversed with timely and adequate care. The Parnia Lab in NYU's Grossman School of Medicine puts it most succinctly:

> The advent of CPR in the 1960s was revolutionary, demonstrating that the heart could potentially be restarted after it had stopped. What had been a clear moment of death was shown to be potentially reversible in some people. What was once called death—the ultimate end point—was now widely called cardiac arrest, and became a starting point. From then on, it was only if someone had requested not to be resuscitated or when CPR was deemed to have failed that a person would be declared dead by "cardiopulmonary criteria." Since the discovery of CPR, physicians have simply shifted the time before irreversible death is declared. However, biologically speaking, cardiac arrest and death by cardiopulmonary criteria are the same process, albeit marked at different points in time depending on when a declaration of death is made.
>
> (Parnia Lab)

In other words, the advancement of medical technology to restart the heart allows cardio-pulmonary death to be viewed as possibly reversible through medical intervention, making brain death the medical gold standard for death in hospital today. This has also led to wide-spread training in the use of CPR, and its application, along with the use of defibrillators to restart hearts and extend lives. This is in addition to the adoption of medical interventions such as pacemakers, which allow doctors to remotely monitor cardiac function.

One unintended consequence of the adoption of CPR, however, has been a lack of informed understanding regarding the possible damage CPR can cause since it often cracks and breaks ribs in the attempt to restart the heart. Additionally, many people are unaware of CPR's low success rate, perhaps as a result of television shows and movies that tend to falsely demonstrate CPR's efficacy. Studies have shown that most people believe that the rates of survival range around 50–75%, when in fact, actual rates of survival after CPR are about 12% for non-hospital cardiac events, and around 25–40% for cardiac events that occur in the hospital. These numbers reveal a large disconnect between popular belief and the usual outcomes regarding CPR. CPR does work sometimes, and especially immediately after cardiac arrest, but positive outcomes are much rarer than negative ones, and even when there is a successful outcome (of the heart restarting), it often does so at the cost of some fairly invasive damage. That being said, the important takeaway here is that cardio-pulmonary innovations have shifted death in the public imagination from something irreversible and permanent to something that might be reversed with timely medical intervention. This shift, however, has also complicated the definition and understanding of death.

Since cardio-pulmonary death is now medically verifiable, death is also primarily a medical event, considered to be something that must be recognized and confirmed before it can be legally official. In other words, medical personnel are not merely the extenders of life, but also the pronouncers of death, and responsible for the legal verification of a death. Legal definitions of death are also important, since they protect the living, the medical profession, and help guide determinations of both the living and the dead. However, each country generally adopts its own definition, and even with countries (such as the United States), there can be variance on how the definition of death is understood and interpreted.

In the United States, the 1981 Uniform Declaration of Death Act, which is used to declare death, states that an individual who has sustained either irreversible cessation of circulatory and respiratory functions (death by cardiorespiratory criteria) or irreversible cessation of all functions of the entire brain, including the brain stem, can be declared dead (death by brain death criteria). Today, due to the reduction in gun crimes and increased use of seatbelts in cars, fewer people suffer permanent brain damage and brain death after traumatic brain injury. Thus, while a very small minority of people are declared dead based on brain death criteria, the vast majority of the population is declared dead based on cardiorespiratory criteria—after the heart stops beating.

(Parnia Lab)

It is important to note here that both of these understandings of death emerged in the last fifty years, which means that death, as it is understood today, is still a fairly new concept. Additionally, as medical technology continues to evolve, it may be more important than ever for people to inform themselves of the difference between cardio-pulmonary, whole brain, and partial brain death.

WHOLE BRAIN AND PARTIAL BRAIN DEATH

Unlike cardio-pulmonary death, **whole brain death** is defined as the irreversible loss of function of the higher brain and the brainstem, which can often be indicated by a permanent loss of consciousness and the loss of a patient's ability to breathe on one's own, requiring the need for permanent medical intervention to sustain the basic body functions (the term "life support" here can be problematic since it leads to false understandings of life, and even death). **Partial brain death** is defined by the cessation in functioning of the brainstem (rather than the entire brain). Both result in permanent and irreversible death, but partial brain death generally requires less costly and less invasive testing to verify the cessation of functioning. The increasing complexity over the definition of death has led to the contemporary utilization of death as defined by brain death—either whole brain or partial brain—death, which is usually only medically verifiable through medical equipment and testing.

Concurrent with the rise in this complexity, however, **organ donation**, the transferal of certain organs and tissues from one person to another (usually from a brain dead person, although some living donations, such as kidney donation, can also be made) further complicates the understanding of who qualifies as living and can be legally declared dead. Transferring vital and singular organs from one person to another requires one person's body to be kept alive in a healthy state, necessitating artificial respiration from ventilators, while the removal of organs and transferal also condemns that body to certain death. In this way, the need to sustain bodies that were considered to be "brain-dead" in order to facilitate organ donation to other bodies unable to function without those organs created a medical impetus in the 1950s and 1960s to normalize brain death. The fact remains that, with rare exceptions, there can be no organ donation without the contemporary definition of **brain death**.

> These two issues-terminating life-sustaining treatment and pro-curing organs from the newly dead-were the explicit impetus for a 1968 report called "A Definition of Irreversible Coma," produced by the Ad Hoc Committee of the Harvard Medical School to Examine the Definition of Brain Death. In this report, the committee spelled out the clinical criteria for determining that a comatose patient was not *merely* comatose and respirator dependent, but that he belonged instead to a smaller, clinically definable class that we would now call "brain dead." These clin-ical criteria included: (1) unreceptivity and unresponsivity to externally applied stimuli and inner need; (2) absence of sponta-neous muscular movements or spontaneous respiration; and (3) no elicitable brainstem reflexes. The report stated that patients who passed these tests should be considered *already dead*, not-withstanding the continued function of their circulatory system. Since they were dead, treatment could be stopped (unilaterally) and organs could be procured even while the heart was still beating, including the heart itself.
>
> (Rubenstein et al, 2006)

These tests, however, rely on advanced medical technology in order to certify brain death, so it is important to note here that countries without broad access to more advanced medical technologies still heavily rely on **cardio-pulmonary definitions of death**.

In addition, class and education disparities become evident when some people have access to organ donation, while others do not, because of a wide variation in medical treatment and its access. On a macro level, more populous and poorer countries generally do not rely on definitions of brain death as their primary definition of death (resulting in less organ donation). One 2015 study found that, "22% of low-income vs 97% of high-income countries had an institutional protocol for brain death determination. The major reasons for the absence of brain death policies were the lack of either expertise or technology" (Wahlster et al, 2015). And even in those countries in which brain death has been adopted as the primary criteria for determining death, there remains a fairly wide variation in how that definition is determined. Practice guidelines vary in the number of physicians required to verify death, the need for additional laboratory testing in order to confirm initial findings, and the types of tests required to affirm brain death.

Additionally, even in economically prosperous countries, the definition of brain death can vary, with countries utilizing socialized systems of medicine tending to adopt less costly and more easily administered tests relying on partial brain death as the quantifying measure of death. Countries such as the United States that rely on private medical systems, and in which the majority of costs are borne by the individual, tend to utilize whole brain death criteria as a way to determine whether a patient is dead. Confirmatory tests such as the EEG are required to confirm brain death, in addition to multiple physicians' signatures to sign off on a death certificate. Thus, even those countries that utilize brain death as their dominant definition of death demonstrate variation as to how death should be determined, and in what ways it should be measured and confirmed.

MORTALITY RATES

Mortality rates are the demographic prediction of death in a population and they are utilized by sociologists, epidemiologists, public health officials, and public safety offices, among others, to predict and understand general death trends. Generally, on a global scale, females have a longer **life expectancy** than males, with the exception of childbearing years, and the risk of death for both males and females is highest in the year immediately after birth, with the first year of life twice the death rate of the next thirteen years combined. The death rate rises again in the years following puberty and these deaths are largely due to accidents, suicides, and homicides. After that, the mortality rate increases incrementally until mid-life, when mortality surpasses the rates in the first year of life. Mortality rates and **life expectancy** are good indicators for broader social factors such as the economic wealth of a country and the quality of medical care that can be found there. Over time, and as countries become economically developed, the life expectancy has increased and mortality rates have decreased. In ancient Rome, for example, the average life expectancy was around twenty eight years, while today in most industrial countries, the average person can expect to live to about seventy eight years. Mortality rates and life expectancy can also reveal issues in the quality of care or economic disparity, as decreases in life expectancy can reveal systemic problems regarding healthcare. For example, in the United States in the Pacific Northwest, infant mortality rates are very low (between 3 and 4%), while in the Deep South, they are high (between 7 and 11%; Center for Disease Control, "Infant Mortality Rates by State,"). Mortality rates can thus help spotlight disparities and reveal where issues need to be addressed.

CONCLUSION

The definition of death—how it is determined, who is qualified to make that determination, and what tests should be utilized to confirm it—is by no means universally understood. The definition of what it means to be dead is also culturally variable, influenced by economic circumstances, medical training, and access to medical equipment and technology. In short, when studying death and dying, we need to first confirm that we all mean the same thing when we talk about death. Last, the advancement of medical technology has not only extended lives but also complicated death—as the lines between life and death have become blurred and one person's death may be required to extend another person's life. Finally, mortality rates—or statistics that allow us to compare rates of death in different populations—are an important indicator of the quality of life. How long one lives, whether one lives, how one dies, and the type of death one dies from are all indicators of the quality of a life one has lived. In Chapter 3, we will turn to examine the ways in which disposal customs and religious imaginaries intersect, illustrating the importance of bodies even after they have died.

REFERENCES

Center for Disease Control, "Infant Mortality Rates by State," https://www.cdc.gov/nchs/pressroom/sosmap/infant_mortality_rates/infant_mortality.htm, last accessed February 14, 2022.

Nahm, Michael, Bruce Greyson, Emily Williams Kelly, and Erlendur Haraldsson. "Terminal lucidity: A review and a case collection." *Archives of Gerontology and Geriatrics* 55, no. 1 (2012): 138–142.

Parnia Lab, NYU Grossman School of Medicine, "From Death to the Rise of Cardiopulmonary Resuscitation," https://med.nyu.edu/research/parnia-lab/about-cardiac-arrest-post-cardiac-arrest-syndrome-death/from-death-to-the-rise-cpr, last accessed May 10, 2022.

Rubenstein, A., Cohen, E., and Jackson, E. *The definition of death and the ethics of organ procurement from the deceased*. President's Council on Bioethics, 2006.

Wahlster, Sarah, Eelco FM Wijdicks, Pratik V. Patel, David M. Greer, J. Claude Hemphill, Marco Carone, and Farrah J. Mateen. "Brain death declaration: practices and perceptions worldwide." *Neurology* 84, no. 18 (2015): 1870–1879.

FOR FURTHER READING

Rubenstein, Alan, Eric Cohen, and Erica Jackson. *The definition of death and the ethics of organ procurement from the deceased*. President's Council on Bioethics, 2006. https://permanent.fdlp.gov/lps92742/rubenstein.html

This is an extremely well-organized and thorough paper written by the President's Council on Bioethics, and includes an excellent discussion of the different definitions of death that occur in modern medicine (including lung, heart, and extensive discussion of the various forms of brain deadness).

Veatch, Robert M., and Lainie Friedman Ross. *Defining Death: The Case for Choice*. Washington DC: Georgetown University Press, 2016. https://baylor.primo.exlibrisgroup.com/discovery/fulldisplay?context=L&vid=01BUL_INST:BAYLOR&search_scope=MyInst_and_CI&tab=Everything&docid=alma991009071189705576

This book studies the definition of death and includes chapters on whole-brain, circulatory (somatic), and higher brain death, while also considering the implications of consciousness and the death donor clause.

Cann, Candi K., and John Troyer. "Trans-Atlantic death methods: Disciplinarity shared and challenged by a common language." *Mortality* 22, no. 2 (2017): 105–117.

This is a good article that explains some of the differences between the United States and the United Kingdom, demonstrating differences impacted by socialized medicine and private medical schemes, including the adoption of whole brain death in the United States and partial brain death in the United Kingdom.

"Death." *Mosby's Medical, Nursing, & Allied Health Dictionary*, Elsevier Inc. (Mosby), 2001. *Gale OneFile: Health and Medicine*, link.gale.com/apps/doc/A173808631/HRCA?u=txshracd2488&sid=bookmark-HRCA&xid=54a3ea42. Accessed 19 Feb. 2022.

This is a brief definition of death both as apparent death and legal death.

Nahm, Michael, Bruce Greyson, Emily Williams Kelly, and Erlendur Haraldsson. "Terminal lucidity: A review and a case collection." *Archives of gerontology and geriatrics* 55, no. 1 (2012): 138–142. doi:10.1016/j.archger.2011.06.031

An interesting and insightful examination of the "last rally" of dying patients.

DISPOSAL

INTRODUCTION

The ways in which bodies are disposed are closely related to after-life imaginaries and our relationship with the body. Whether bodies are burned, buried, frozen, freeze-dried, composted, or donated largely depends on what we believe happens to us after we die and the ways in which the body in this life is necessary for any afterlives we imagine. In addition, environmental pollution, land scarcity, disposition costs, and other concerns of the living pressure people to create new and innovative ways of disposing of the dead. For example, because of its affordability and land-saving nature, cremation has rapidly surpassed burial as the preferred method of body disposal in the twenty-first century and religious authorities have needed to adapt to this shift or risk losing their adherents. This chapter discusses the various methods of preparation of the corpse following death, and the many disposition options, in addition to highlighting various religious attitudes and practices around the world.

THE DEAD BODY: CORPSE PRESERVATION

Embalmment, the preservation of the dead body through chemicals in order to delay the natural and visual signs of death, is often utilized by funeral homes when there is going to be a visitation before the cremation or the funeral service, itself, as it is one way that the funeral home can maximize their control over the corpse and minimize unwanted noises or movements of the corpse during

DOI: 10.4324/9780429025075-3

a viewing or a service. Many people mistakenly believe that not embalming presents a social hazard, while the opposite is true; the chemicals involved in embalmment are extremely toxic and embalmers are required by law to wear full body protection and a respirator while embalming. However, part of the success in selling embalmment services to consumers is predicated on the notion that corpses, themselves, are inherently unhygienic and present a danger to society.

Embalmment has a long history, from upper class Egyptians several thousand years ago to various royalty and rulers throughout history, but in the United States, the practice of embalmment became standard during and following the American Civil War in 1861–1865, when embalmment served to preserve the bodies of the dead soldiers so that they could be returned home for burial. Embalmment drains the corpse of all of its bodily fluids, replacing these fluids with a preservative fluid treated so that it will help make the body more pliant to the touch, slow down decomposition, and bring underlying color to the skin (often the fluids are dyed so as to provide the skin with underlying color). Additionally, embalmment also involves the stuffing of the cheeks with cotton (which sink after a person has died), wiring the mouth shut (so it won't accidentally open during visitation), placing plastic eye caps or more cotton under the eyelids (to round out the eyes and keep them from accidentally opening), arranging the corpse (which sometimes means massaging or wiring the limbs into place), and applying makeup on a corpse so that its pallor can be made lifelike once again. Additionally, small plugs are placed in the cavities of the body to prevent leakage or sounds from escaping the body during visitation. Embalmment is extremely unnatural and incredibly invasive, and what started as a practical necessity to allow for the preservation of the body for burial has turned into a standard practice in many funerals.

The main reason for embalming's continued popularity in the American death care industry is threefold—(1) it is a service with a wide profit margin, and as a result, funeral homes often sell it as an integral part of the funeral service package, (2) it allows the funeral home to offer visitations and viewings with much more flexibility in regards to scheduling times, and (3) it allows for the pliant cooperation of the deceased so that there are no awkward moments (noises, movement, etc.) of the corpse during the viewing or funeral service itself. These reasons behind embalmment, however, have been largely under-emphasized, and as a result, many people instead view embalmment as an essential part of the funeral service.

Despite the supposed practicality behind the increase in the practice of embalmment, it is not practiced in many religions—namely Judaism, Islam, Buddhism, and Hinduism, and yet, it is commonly practiced among Christians residing in North America. This tendency is in part because of religious worldviews, afterlife beliefs, and imagined embodiment, which have been both perpetuated by, and capitalized upon, by the death care industry. This is not to say that all those who embalm are Christians; rather, that the practice of embalmment seems to utilize Christian symbolism and language that underscores and privileges Christian rhetoric, to the extent that embalming is largely accepted and practiced in Christian circles (with exceptions, of course—Dutch Reform, Amish Americans, and Jehovah's Witness, for example, are among those who do not practice embalming in their communities). Before moving into an exploration of Christians and embalming, however, I will briefly explore the religious viewpoints of those who generally reject the practice of embalmment (one must note here that, even in embalmment, there are exceptions).

THE JEWISH PREPARATION OF THE BODY

Jews prefer to bury the deceased immediately and do not embalm the body or condone its viewing, considering it to be disrespectful to the deceased. For this reason, Jewish services for the dead are usually held as soon as possible after the death of a person. Preparation of the dead body proceed according to Ecclesiastes 5:14, in which it is written, "As he came, so should he go" (Funeral Practices Committee of The Board of Rabbis of Southern California, n.d., p. 3). Thus, when a person dies, their body is washed and purified just as they were when they were born. **Taharah** is the traditional Jewish act of washing and purifying the body and is generally performed by a person trained in the traditional Jewish purification rituals. Men wash and purify men and women wash and purify women. Usually the body is washed with warm water from head to toe, taking care to never turn the body face down. The most meaningful aspect of these rituals is their communal aspect—at no point is the deceased left on their own following their death. From dying to death to burial, the Jewish community accompanies the deceased in their journey.

After the body has been washed and purified, the body is dressed in a traditional white shroud, known as a **tachrichim**. Jewish people are never buried in their traditional clothes but in a white shroud made of linen or muslin. The idea behind this is that in Judaism, all are found equal in death, and therefore no person is deemed better than another, so that even in death, one should be buried in a humble manner. The white shroud is symbolic of equality in life through death (in other words, though one may be materially successful in life, in death, all are dead). In addition, usually the shroud is hand-sewn so that the stiches will easily disintegrate; if the shroud is machine-sewn, usually someone will rip some of the seams of the burial shroud so that it disintegrates easier. The tachrichim is so important to Jewish burial custom that if one is not found to dress the body, then the funeral will be postponed until one can be obtained. Jewish men are also buried with their prayer shawl, the **tallit**, a traditional fringed shawl that is usually used by Jewish men during prayer. Before burial, one of the fringes of the prayer shawl will be cut so that it is rendered ineffective. If the deceased did not own a tallit, then usually one is found and provided for the burial. Genesis 3:19 ("By the sweat of your brow you will eat your food until you return to the ground, since from it you were taken for dust you are and to dust you will return," (NIV Study Bible) states that the proper cycle for the deceased is to return to dust, and for this reason, it is preferable for a Jew to be buried directly into the ground in a burial shroud.

The Jewish cosmological view of the afterlife varies from branch to branch and person to person, with some Jews believing in a place called **Sheol**, where all the dead, both righteous and unrighteous, go after their death. Like most faiths, however, individual Jews vary in their understandings of the afterlife. Some have believed in a resurrection, others in reincarnation, while finally, other Jews reject the notion of the afterlife altogether, or simply see it as irrelevant, stating that their purpose is life itself and a relationship with God in *this* life. For most Jews, though, observing God's command to return the body to dust is also an acknowledgement of God's role in the Jewish cycle of life from creation to death. Thus, embalming is not customarily practiced in the Jewish community and is generally frowned upon.

THE MUSLIM PREPARATION OF THE BODY

Islam also rejects embalmment and the deceased is usually buried within twenty-four hours of death, except in the case of practical constraints (such as when the coroner or medical examiner cannot be reached to sign the death certificate or an autopsy needs to be performed). Like Judaism, in Islam, women wash and purify the female bodies for burial and men prepare the men. Many Muslim cemeteries have rooms for the preparation and washing of the body before death. As in Judaism, there is no visitation or viewing and embalming is not merely rejected but considered unnecessary, only allowed when required by law. If there is a need to delay a funeral, generally the deceased is refrigerated for preservation services, but this is an extremely rare practice. In the Qur'an, it is written (رَاجِعونَ إِلَيْهِ وَإِنَّـا للهِ إِنَّا) "Inna lillahi wa inna ilayhi raji'un" "Indeed we belong to Allah, and indeed to Him we will return" (Qur'an, Surah 2, verse 156), and this verse is recited immediately upon learning of a death. Muslims believe that all go to a final judgment before God, and one's afterlife is dependent on the outcome of that judgment. Death in Islam is viewed as a passage between two segments of one continuous life. For the observant Muslim, death is not viewed negatively but as an opportunity to be close to God. Because of this view, unnecessary life extension through the use of life support when the quality of life is poor is viewed negatively, and is usually denied. Conversely, euthanasia is not condoned because life is a gift from God and the willing taking of such life would be a grievous sin. Autopsies and embalming are also not permitted and are considered to be unnecessarily invasive, disrespecting the sacrality of the body, which belongs to God.

Because Muslim burials usually occur within twenty-four hours following a death, most mosques have burial committees who volunteer to ritually wash and shroud the body and prepare it for burial. The ritual washers are divided by gender who wash the body three times in water, before applying perfume to the deceased.

Unless the person is considered to be a martyr (in which case they are buried in the clothes they died in and not washed), the deceased is washed and then placed in a white shroud consisting of five pieces for women and three pieces for men. Directions are an essential part of the Muslim faith, and following a death, the deceased is turned to face Mecca and buried in that direction either in a simple wooden box or on their right side in a shroud. After the body has been covered with soil, it is customary for each person to throw three handfuls of dirt onto the grave, saying "From the earth did God create you." This is quite similar to the Jewish custom of throwing dirt on the grave and allows the community to take part in the burial of the deceased, while acknowledging that death is a part of life.

In both Judaism and Islam, there is no viewing or visitation because it is considered to be disrespectful to God. Excessive mourning is also discouraged as it can be a sign that one has not submitted oneself to, and respected, the will of God who has decreed the time and place of death for the deceased. Both Judaism and Islam have strict proscriptions prohibiting the cutting of flesh (tattooing for example) and thus invasive practices involving the body are considered violations of God's creation. This belief thus extends to embalmment, viewed as invasive and unnecessary. It is significant that the Jewish and Muslim proscriptions against embalming have not influenced the contemporary Christian tradition. Finally, views on organ donation vary and are somewhat culturally (not only religiously) dependent. The sale of organs is never permitted, but there seems to be some variation in whether organ donation may be allowed, variable depending on culture (e.g., among Indian Muslims, organ donation is not permitted, while some Middle Eastern Islamic countries view organ donations from one person to another as a gift of life and a blessing from God). Even in organ donation, though, there seems to be a stress on the preference for Muslim to Muslim donation, and only in the case of saving a life endangered by death.

THE HINDU PREPARATION OF THE BODY

In Hinduism, as in Judaism, Islam, and Buddhism, the body is washed and dressed in burial clothes for the funerary pyre. During the washing of the body—known as the **abhishekam** or holy bath—the head should face south and the body is washed in a mixture of milk, yogurt, ghee (clarified butter), and honey to soften and perfume the body. Then the body is washed with purified water, the big toes are tied together, the hands placed in a prayer position, and it is shrouded in a sheet and/or a simple wooden box for the short wake before the cremation. During the wake, it is customary for a picture of the deceased person's favorite deity to be placed near the head, along with a small oil lamp, and friends and family will pay their respects. In India, it is customary to burn a body near a river, so that the soul has access to the purification and cleansing nature of the water. Hindus living in the United States, however, generally opt to cremate at the crematorium with close family members present, followed by a memorial service at the temple, and then finally a scattering of ashes in the ocean of the United States, or the ashes are sometimes also reserved and transported back to India for scattering at a later time. In Hinduism, embalmment is generally rejected and the body is cremated within twenty four to forty eight hours. In both Hinduism and Buddhism embalmment is deemed unnecessary, as the body is cremated, and the cremation occurs very quickly following the death. Both Buddhism and Hinduism believe in the cycle of life, death, and rebirth, and cremating the bodies allows for practitioners to burn their bodies and free the souls for preparation to move into the next life. Buddhism and Hinduism reject the practice of embalmment, though their reasons for rejecting embalming as a practice vary.

THE SIKH PREPARATION OF THE BODY

When a Sikh dies, the funeral is usually planned within three days of the death, and cremation rather than burial is generally preferred, though if cremation is not possible, burial is permitted. There are a few key rules concerning the dying process, which include not moving a person as they are dying from their bed, and the importance of reciting prayers centered on focusing one's consciousness on Waheguru, or God. After a person has died, they are generally washed and changed, placed into clothes, along with the Five Ks that demonstrate Sikh identity. If they have died in the hospital, then usually the body is brought home or to a funeral home where it can be properly washed and dressed in preparation for the funeral. Usually, the washing of the body is performed by older members of the family or friends and will be of the same gender as the deceased. First, the body and hair are washed with yoghurt, in order to soften the skin, and then with soap and warm water to cleanse the deceased. While they are being washed and dressed, usually people will chant God's name over and over or recite a prayer that affirms the oneness of God (the **Gurmantar Waheguru** or **Mul Mantar**), or both. The body is then redressed in clean clothes and adorned with orange and white chrysan-themums, considered to be mourning flowers in India. If possi-ble, on the day of the funeral, the body may be taken home for a short time (15–20 minutes) and prayers recited by either a priest or another religious leader. The funeral itself is known as **Antam Sanskaar**, which translates as "last rite," and usually takes place at a **gurudwara**, or a Sikh temple. Before the funeral, Sikh commu-nity leaders gather to recite from Sikh texts for forty eight hours in the presence of the deceased, much like Catholics might hold a rosary or a wake for their dead before burial. For funerals, partic-ipants are expected to remove their shoes, cover their head, and refrain from weeping as much as possible, because the funeral is seen as an opportunity for the deceased to return to God.

THE BUDDHIST PREPARATION OF THE BODY

In Buddhism, most people prefer to be cremated, and generally, like both Judaism and Islam, the body is prepared and washed, usu-ally in the home of the deceased in the presence of family and close friends. The body is then dressed for burial, offerings are made, and the body is prepared for its final resting place. Though Buddhist disposal rites vary by country and sectarian branch, generally a Buddhist undertaker comes to the family's home to prepare the body for cremation, burial, or excarnation (in the case of Tibetan Buddhism). Buddhists believe the soul lingers near the body for days following the death and often the body is not prepared for final dis-position until it is cold. Absolute respect must be given to the body until it its final resting place and often the body is treated as though it is still alive; this is why bodies are not generally embalmed, only washed. That being said, there is generally no proscription against either embalming or organ donation. Buddhism has many folk tales and ghost stories regarding souls that come back to haunt the living because proper care was not taken with their dead bodies. When the body is then cremated, the eldest son (or occasionally in contemporary times, daughter) is called upon to light the funerary pyre or push the crematory button to begin the cremation process. In Buddhism, the lighting of the cremation flame is considered to be the second and final death.

CHINESE PREPARATION OF THE BODY

In China, there is an old saying that the most important thing in life is to be buried well, and this is because the afterlife in Chinese Religion replicates this world. How one is cared for in death, and then remembered after, is believed to directly impact one's afterlife. The funeral is not only an opportunity for a family to demonstrate their status and social standing in their community, but is also a religious ritual in which the deceased is transformed into an ancestor who can look after and provide for the living. The concept of reciprocity between the realm of the living and the dead is paramount in religious rituals surrounding the dead. Proper care for the dead is very important in Chinese society, and the living will go to great lengths to demonstrate proper care for the dead not just at the funeral, but for years afterward in holidays honoring the dead (**qing ming**), in which burial sites are regularly cleaned and regular offerings of food, prayers, and incense are made to and on behalf of the dead. Because of this, death can be viewed as not merely an important time, but dead bodies can be viewed as dangerous and **polluting** (the belief that one can be harmed or made unclean) if they are not properly cared for. This accounts for the many superstitions that have arisen surrounding the care of and disposal for the dead (for example if someone has died at home in an apartment building or small community, many people will place a mirror on their door so that the deceased ghost will see themselves in the mirror and become frightened and run away).

Embalming is not generally practiced because it is viewed as expensive and unnecessary, though the Chinese were not unfamiliar with corpse preservation after death. The corpse of Mao Zedong is one whose body was preserved and placed in state for perpetual observation like other Communist leaders (Lenin and Stalin in the former USSR and Ho Chi Minh in Vietnam) and can still be viewed today in Beijing's Tiananmen Square. Mao is the exception, though, rather than the rule, and most people are not embalmed. After death, the body is washed and dressed in special clothes. The corpse is usually washed several times in order to ritually purify the corpse—three times in Taiwan and seven to eight times in mainland China. Often a coin is placed in the mouth of the deceased along with rice in order for the deceased to bribe the officials of the Chinese **underworld** in the Chinese afterlife so that they will not be hungry in their afterlife. Other personal items are often buried or burned with the deceased, and/or cardboard replicas of all the things the dead will need in the afterlife are burned with them so that they have all that they might need in their afterlife. A passport to the underworld can also be included in the coffin or with the person, so that they can easily gain access into the Chinese underworld.

Along with the preparation of the body, additional arrangements are made for the transferal of an aspect of the soul from the deceased's body into a wooden tablet, which will then be moved to the family altar where it will be the recipient of prayers on behalf of the deceased. The family of the deceased breathe their life force onto a writing brush, which is then dipped into vermillion ink symbolizing blood, and a dot is placed on a small wooden tablet with the name of the deceased. Often a picture of the deceased is placed on the tablet as well, and this tablet then becomes the physical embodiment of the deceased remaining in this world. Until the corpse is safely buried or cremated, however, it remains a dangerous and polluting element for the world of the living and special care must be taken to propitiate and watch over the deceased.

INDIGENOUS DISPOSAL TRADITIONS

Indigenous disposal traditions vary widely, but generally favor natural burial and/or disposal, because of the importance placed on the natural world. Native Hawai'ians were historically buried under small stone mounds, while others were buried in sand dunes or in the ground. If a person was a high chief, or a person of high honor, sometimes the remains would be buried at night to conceal their location, since it was believed that the remains of a person contained spiritual power that could be harnessed (for both good and bad).

Some people even planted foods near the bones of the deceased, since they believed that food fertilized by the dead would bestow the **mana**, or spiritual power, of the dead onto the food. Today, people are usually buried in traditional cemeteries, or sometimes cremated and disposed of in paddle out ceremonies in which people gather in canoes or surfboards to dispose of the dead. Recently, there has been a movement to re-instill the traditional practice of partial cremation, wrapping the bones of a deceased Hawai'ian person in sacred cloth and placing them in a burial container in a cemetery.

Cherokee burial traditions generally do not permit autopsies as they are considered invasive and disruptive, and it is generally believed that the spirit will not be able to begin its journey properly. Most simply, a body is usually shrouded in a white sheet, after being washed with ceremonial herbs (often lavender) that both purify and cleanse, before being placed in a casket, usually with small gifts like a feather that have spiritual significance. It is customary to spend several days honoring the death of someone who has died and the burial ceremony usually involves the entire community. Now, because many Native Americans are also Christians, there may be a sort of syncretistic funeral, in which both Native American and Christian traditions are observed. Similarly, Inuits practice both land burial and sea disposal, because the tundra is often frozen, making land disposal challenging. If opting for burial, Inuits generally bury their dead in cemeteries near or on their settlements, and have never practiced embalming because of their care and respect of the natural world, in which humans are also a participant.

THE CHRISTIAN PREPARATION OF THE BODY: IMAGINED EMBODIMENT IN CHRISTIANITY[1]

The practice of embalming then cannot be strictly confined to cultural geography and the socio-cultural influences of American culture. Nor, however, can the practice of embalming be directly linked to Christian belief systems, as many Christians in Europe and Latin America do not widely embalm the deceased. Orthodox Christians—because of the long wakes generally involved in the funeral process—often do embalm their deceased, though cremation is strictly forbidden. The question then remains—why do North American Christians embalm more than their Christian counterparts in other countries, and why does this group, more than any other religious group in the United States, prefer to embalm their dead, even though practitioners of other religions have generally resisted the larger cultural trend toward embalmment?

The importance of the embalmed body is that it is simultaneously the actor, and the acted upon, it is the subject and the object, the deceased, yet no longer fully human, dead, yet not-dead. The embalmed corpse, devoid of its organs and its fluids, stuffed and sewn, is now an actor with a part in a ritual of mourning meant to comfort those who encounter the body in its newly sterilized and purified form. The embalmed body functions as both a realization of the past and a projection of anticipated future. It operates as a bridge between reality and the imagined, its artificial corporeality reinforcing the place of tension between death and the afterlife. If the body can continue to play a vital role in the community without its organs, without its owner operating its body, then perhaps an afterlife becomes possible as well.

In early and medieval Christianity, one of the signs of favor with God was the preservation of the corpse. Considered a miracle, many saints were identified through the lack of deterioration of their corpse and were labeled as **incorrupt corpses**, corpses that demonstrated little or no decay following their death, the integrity of the skin linked to the integrity of the soul. Incorrupt corpses are known by their sweet odor (the "odor of sanctity") and their lack of decomposition. Many incorrupt corpses were discovered because of dreams or miracles, and upon being dug up from the ground, revealed to be intact. The top feature of an incorrupt corpse is the corpse's pliability and they are often placed on display in churches, hands folded in prayer, or even sitting in prayer. Incorrupt corpses often became some of the more popular figures in the Catholic Church, as they gave people a sense of hope regarding their own afterlives. The rotting of bodily flesh was often linked to the soul's time in purgatory—a visible window into the events going on in the afterlife, and those corpses that stayed intact were believed to be evidence of God's favor and afterlife. The preservation of the body thus has a history in Christianity of being associated with the afterlife.

However, in stark contrast to this view of embodied sanctity, early American Puritans focused on the separation of this life and the next, arguing that death was a natural fact of life and burials should be handled stoically and as a matter of course. The body was viewed not as an earthly window into the afterlife but as an impediment to it. Puritan funerals buried the body quickly as the focus of the funeral service was to bring one closer to God, through the acceptance of his will. American Protestant evangelicals thus utilized the corpse as a way to move away from the more austere practices of the Puritans, but the corpse that became center stage in this religious culture was not the decomposing body, but the sterile, cosmetic, and embalmed one. In describing the afterlife, Christians often recall the bible verse of 1 Corinthians 15:54-56, "When the perishable has been clothed with the imperishable, and the mortal with immortality, then the saying that is written will come true: 'Death has been swallowed up in victory (NIV Study Bible).'" Death that appears as life through the embalmed body became a symbol of the evangelical victory over death itself and can be viewed as a foretaste of the afterlife to come. The popularity of embalming as a service in American funerals is not merely the result of cultural forces or purely interpreted by religious beliefs; both the exponential growth of the funeral home industry as a private industry and the medicalization and professionalization of dying and death are also to be taken into account. The privatization of American industry and American denominationalism went hand in hand to create a ripe consumer culture in which funeral directors were able to effectively create a cultural rhetoric surrounding death and grief, in which embalming became a symbol of American progress, modernity, success, and the manipulation of time (corpses that can wait on the living vs. the other way around), bodies, and space. Only Christians sanction and accept embalmment as a regular (and even important) part of deathcare services. In comparison to other faiths, the eschatology of Christianity seems to privilege the need for the body to *appear* alive, even if doing so requires highly artificial and invasive means. It is no different with casket and disposal choices.

CASKETS AND CEMETERIES

Casket choices are another consumer death good affected by religious worldviews, and today, there is a rich assortment of casket choices available on the market. Once more commonly known as coffins, the term **coffin** was changed to **casket** by the funeral home industry to indicate a box, such as a jewelry box, that holds something precious and of value. In this way, the funeral home industry succeeded in domesticating the term coffin to a term that implied delicacy, emphasizing the preciousness of the contents rather than the ugly reality of the death. Funeral homes have also become more inventive in the last forty years as well, offering innovations on caskets that include everything from interchangeable corners, to casket lid inserts and cap panels, to liner rentals. Innovations in caskets have been popular in the last twenty years with companies like Crazy Coffins (n.d., https://www.crazycoffins.co.uk/) offering custom-built caskets that look more like art installations than coffins. Caskets come in a wide variety of materials, ranging from cardboard to metal, and the price variation is equally wide, ranging from hundreds of dollars to tens of thousands. Internet and retail distributors have also moved into the casket market, with everyone from Amazon to Walmart offering coffins on the cheap. A keyword search on Amazon for caskets returns thousands of available choices, with caskets available for people and/or pets.

Cemeteries have undergone many changes in the North American landscape in the last two hundred and fifty years. Once occupying a privileged place in city centers, near important churches and houses of government, many cemeteries have been banished to the outskirts of city suburbs, or dug up, moved, and replaced with a contemporary landscape. Cemeteries are not merely repositories of the dead, but architectural and symbolic intersections of two worldviews—the one of the living, and the hopes and thoughts surrounding death and what death is and what it should be. The tomb of the unknown soldier at the Arlington National Cemetery in the United States, for example, serves to reinforce a deeper cultural message that all the dead who lose their lives in the service of nationalistic interests will be remembered as heroic (similarly, Yasukuni Shrine in Tokyo serves a similar function for Japan's war-dead). Cemeteries also map the world of the living, with religious cemeteries interring their members in sacred ground, while outsiders are buried elsewhere. Finally, cemeteries reflect class and status, with tombstones and vaults reflecting the status and material success (or lack thereof) of the person who has died. In the United States, most cemeteries are privately owned and run, which means that they have their own rules and regulations regarding burial. In burial, as in life, people often want to be buried with those they identify with—either in class, religious persuasion, or in demographics—and one of the first actions of the many diasporic groups we find in the United States is the purchase of burial ground. Thus, there are Buddhist, Jewish, Muslim, Catholic, Orthodox, and Protestant burial grounds, along with cemeteries that specialize in ethnic subsections of these groups, like African American Protestants or Latin/x Catholics.

JEWISH BURIAL AND DISPOSAL

Though some cemeteries do not permit direct burial of the body, if a casket must be used, it is preferred that the casket be made of wood with no designs or metal ornamentation. Some Jewish communities contend that even metal nails or brackets may not be utilized in the construction of a casket because metal is the material for weapons of war. Similarly, the inside of the coffin must be plain and unlined with no ornamentation or decoration. The most popular choice in caskets for Jews remains the simple pine box, which generally varies in price from around $400–$600. Pine is considered not to be ostentatious, and because it is natural wood, will allow rapid decomposition in the ground; sometimes, breaking the box right before it is buried is done to encourage even faster decomposition of the bodily remains.

Most Jews have their own cemeteries (when Jews first immigrated to the United States, it was often the first thing they bought) and still opt to be buried there. Jewish tradition claims that all should attend the interment of the body for both psychological and religious reasons. Viewing the final interment of the body is considered the final act of kindness one can perform for the deceased, since it is a kindness that cannot be reciprocated (Funeral Practices Committee of The Board of Rabbis of Southern California, n.d., p. 5). Often, attendees to the burial are expected to place dirt on top of the casket if they cannot actually bury the body themselves, and this act is seen as beneficial for both the deceased and the bereaved. Last, it is not uncommon for a Jew to request that his casket be broken to speed the decomposition process, if he cannot be buried in a shroud alone.

Unlike some traditions, Judaism prefers to stress the world of the living and not the dead, which generally means that a belief in dead spirits, prayers to the dead, or private conversations with the dead are strongly discouraged because they are believed to be too similar to a worship of the dead. That being said, Judaism stresses the need for a balance "that people should avoid the extremes of constant visitation on the one hand, and of complete disregard on the other" (Lamm, n.d.). Thus, some visitation is permitted, particularly on days of distress, anniversaries of the death, etc., as long as these visitations do not occur on a Jewish holy day when one should instead be focused on worshipping God.

MUSLIM BURIAL AND DISPOSAL

Muslims bury their dead in white muslin shrouds following the washing of the body, burying them directly in the ground in the cemetery. The exception to this is the Muslim martyr, who is buried immediately in the ground in the clothes in which s/he was killed without being washed first. Muslim martyrs are not prepared for burial because their presence in the afterlife is assured through their sacrificial death, and therefore they do not need the same preparation for burial (remember, the preparation for burial in the Muslim worldview is for the benefit of the dead not the living). The average Muslim is washed three times by members of the same sex, in the following order: upper right side, upper left side, lower right side, lower left side. A woman's hair is then separated and braided into three parts, and she is dressed in a sleeveless dress and veil. All bodies are shrouded in white sheets bound by one rope at the head, two on the body, and one on the feet, and then transported to the mosque for prayers before being buried. After the community recites prayers, the body is then transported to the cemetery for burial. Generally, communities in the United States do not allow for direct burial without a casket, and thus in the United States, Muslims will purchase a simple, non-ornamental box, often purchasing them from Orthodox Jewish suppliers of death goods, who already make plain pine coffins. Because both Jews and Muslims choose to forgo embalmment, caskets are closed and simple, and made of biodegradable materials (Malek, 2006).

Muslims are generally buried on their right side, perpendicular to Mecca, so that the deceased is facing Mecca. The burial itself cannot take place during sunrise, high noon, or sunset, so generally burials are held in the mid-morning or afternoon. Only men are allowed to be present at the burial itself, and after digging a hole of approximately 1.7 meters, the body is inserted by the male members of the deceased's family. The ropes at the head and the feet are untied by the men and stones or wood (if there is no casket) are placed on top of the deceased in order to prevent direct contact with the soil that will fill the grave, being careful to keep the deceased on their right side. Practically, this also allows for the dirt to uniformly fill the grave so that it will not collapse in on the body. A small marker is placed as an identity marker and the grave is usually slightly raised above the rest of the ground so that people will not accidentally walk on the grave, but no ostentatious markers may be placed on the grave (Muslim Funeral Services, Ltd., n.d.).

CEMETERY COSTS FOR JEWS AND MUSLIMS

The main costs for final disposal among Jews and Muslims in North America, then, is the purchase and maintenance of land for body disposal. Buying cemetery land is usually one of the first major purchases of synagogues and mosques, though at times, some communities have chosen to purchase small plots of burial land within a larger cemetery already in use, especially if the community is small and doesn't have access to the necessary labor required to assist in burial. Larger communities, like the Muslim and Jewish communities in New York and Washington DC, for example, have been able to pool their resources and purchase large tracts of land dedicated to the exclusive use of that particular religious group (e.g., the largest Muslim cemetery in the United States is located in Virginia; see the All Muslim Association of America website in References: All Muslim Association of America (AMAA). n.d.; visit the International Jewish Cemetery Project website in References for a list of Jewish American cemeteries; International Association of Jewish Genealogical Societies. n.d.). Average costs in Muslim cemeteries for burial and maintenance vary according to land costs but remain relatively low. Jewish burial services vary much more in price and can be much more expensive, as Jewish families are much more dispersed than the Muslim population, but also are allowed to have more elaborate headstones and grave markers, which can elevate the price of a burial quite markedly.

CHINESE BURIAL

Even though the Chinese diaspora is located all over the world, there are some core elements that can be pointed to in issues of final disposition. In mainland China, because of land shortage and environmental concerns, cremation is encouraged, and the state helps in the funding of final disposition and the maintenance of columbariums (though there are still those who go out of their way to avoid these state-imposed mandates and purchase land in the countryside in order to bury their dead). In places like Taiwan and Singapore, there is a little more leeway in terms of funeral disposition, though even there, land shortages have caused a variety of disposal methods that are both innovative and at times challenging for traditional Chinese views of death and the afterlife.

Generally, before burial, there is a large feast held for the community that serves to simultaneously feed and nourish the dead as they prepare for their final journey into the underworld. Traditional foods and alcohol are offered and foods such as uncooked rice and twice-cooked pork are offered at the funeral feast along with wine. The feast has the dual function of displaying the wealth and status of the deceased and their family in the community, while also ensuring that the deceased is satiated and will not bring bad luck to the community. Following this feast, there is a large funeral procession accompanying the casket to its burial place. The casket is stuffed with **spirit money** and any other necessary items the deceased might need in their afterlife, before being tightly sealed with caulking and nails. In the procession accompanying the casket to its burial, mourners wear white, carry pictures of the deceased, and hold lights or lanterns in order to ensure that the deceased does not get lost along the way. Loud funeral music is played as a way to keep the deceased entertained and make sure they know where they are going. Finally, more spirit money, paper money printed for use in the spirit world and used to buy things in the afterlife, is burned to aid the deceased person in their journey to the underworld, and ensure they are able to properly bribe the underworld officials, and to rid the streets of any beggar ghosts that might inhibit the deceased person's journey. The ideal place of burial is in the opposite direction of a hill or a mountain and waters flowing in front of the grave, but this is largely dependent on the local environment.

CATHOLIC, ORTHODOX, AND PROTESTANT BURIAL

Catholic casket choices emphasize the notion of **purgatory**, a liminal state for the soul in which one's sins can be forgiven through **intercessory prayer**, prayer on behalf of another person, and the recitation of the rosary. Casket choices emphasize the belief in purgatory through the inclusion of memory drawers and cap panels on caskets. **Memory drawers** allow for the family of the deceased to include letters, prayers, pictures, icons, prayer cards, and rosaries in a concealed drawer of the casket (although one funeral director I interviewed noted that jewelry and other personal trinkets were also frequently included as well), allowing the deceased to be buried with items meant to aid them in their journey to the afterlife. For Protestants, the emphasis is placed on the Do-It-Yourself (DIY) aspects of the funeral, and grieving families encouraged to place personal mementos that the deceased cherished in the drawers. Along with memory drawers, casket lid inserts and cap panels are also popular among Catholic grievers, with customizable "scrapbook" style cap panels that allow for grievers to place letters, pictures, prayer cards, icon pictures, and other mementos in the cap panel of the casket. These differ slightly from the memory drawers in that they are public and on display (if the casket is open), and therefore the messages might not be as private in nature. Catholic material culture is important to these consumer death choices, as the Catholic view of the embodied sacred found in material objects means that they are much more likely to see a need to give the deceased religious objects that might help them in their afterlife.

For Orthodox Christians, caskets are made in a traditional six-sided style out of wood, decorated with the Orthodox cross, which has three crossbeams, with an unhinged top that can be completely removed for the wake. This is so that the family and friends of the deceased can easily reach the deceased for the "Kiss of Peace and Anointing," during which church members stroll by the deceased and offer a kiss to the icon or cross laid on the person who has died. Along with the placement of the icon in the casket, a small bowl of **koliva**, a traditional dish made of boiled wheat and honey and symbolizing the cycle of life and the sweetness of heaven, is usually placed near the head of the deceased, and a candle inserted in the bowl, and lit. Once the mourners have all kissed the icon and the candle is extinguished, the top of the casket is affixed and the body taken to be buried.

Caskets, themselves, are also indicative of religious worldviews, as metal caskets, especially those marketed as hermetically sealed, tend to be most popular with those who choose to embalm their dead out of a fear of bodily deterioration or a desire to preserve the body because of a belief in an embodied afterlife. It is not merely a belief in an embodied afterlife, however, but actually an imagined embodiment that drives the consumer to choose embalmment and hermetically sealed caskets for burial. Ironically, hermetically sealed caskets *increase* the rate of decomposition (though many believe otherwise) because they prevent the air and water and other natural elements from entering the coffin and the body itself is actually the center of the decomposition process. They do, however, seal any disease and contamination inside the coffin, preventing spread of disease. Thus, these caskets, like embalmment, also play on the modern fears of contamination and contagion of dead bodies and are often marketed in the funeral home industry as the best way to preserve the body. Now that we have examined embalmment and burial practices across religious traditions, we will now turn to other popular disposal methods in the contemporary world.

CREMATION

Cremation, a method of corpse disposal that relies on the burning of bodies, either in a crematorium or in an open-air pyre, is the method most commonly used after burial. It is often preferred as a more environmentally friendly (though far less environmentally friendly if the body has been first embalmed, and not as environmentally friendly as natural burial, resomation, or composting). In industrialized countries, cremation takes place in a cremation chamber, or retort, in which a coffin or container (usually made of cardboard or thin wood) is placed inside a chamber powered by natural gas or oil and subject to intense heat of 1,500–2,100 degrees Fahrenheit (around 1,000 degrees centigrade) until the body is reduced to ashes. The process generally takes from one to four hours depending on the weight and size of the body. Afterward, the bone residue is taken out and placed in a pulverizer to reduce the remaining bone fragments to a uniform size and all ash and pulverized bones are returned to the family and friends of the deceased.

Cremation has a long history of acceptance and utilization in Buddhism, Hinduism, and Sikhism— religions in which there is a common belief in reincarnation— and more than three quarters of the population in India cremate their dead, while in Japan over 99% of people are cremated. Conversely, Chinese religions traditionally preferred **inhumation**, or burial, but because of land shortages, the governments in China, Taiwan, and Singapore have generally encouraged the adoption of cremation, and today nearly one half of all mainland Chinese are cremated, while in both Taiwan and Singapore almost all are cremated. Cremation has been slower to be universally adopted in Christian countries, but because of its affordability and the church's more flexible position on cremation, the adoption of cremation as a disposal method is growing exponentially. Today in the United States, nearly half of all people are cremated, while in the United Kingdom, about three-quarters of people choose cremation. In Europe, cremation is widely adopted in the Nordic countries and is slowly gaining more acceptance in southern Europe, where Catholicism remains heavily prevalent. Though traditionally resistant to cremation as a disposal option, in 2016, the papacy announced that cremation could be a viable option for Catholics as long as they interred the remains in a sacred place and did not scatter them. Conversely, Eastern Orthodoxy continues to oppose cremation as a viable disposal option.

CREMAIN DISPOSITION

One benefit of cremation as a disposition method is that the **cremains**, or ashes, can be divided between loved ones and that they are easily re-purposed into various memorial objects. While some people scatter cremains in favorite places of the deceased (in an ocean or in a park, for example), cremains can also be placed into **urns**, or containers filled with the ashes, that can then be stored in a communal location such as a columbarium. A **columbarium** is a structure for the respectful storage of remains, usually in public places such as graveyards, burial grounds, or religious places of worship. Because of their versatile nature, cremains can also be mixed in with cement and turned into off-shore burial sea reefs, aiding in environmental efforts to rebuild sea reefs for fish and other ocean creatures. This has become a particularly popular option in ocean-facing areas such as Hong Kong, Singapore, or Florida, and is one way in which to combine nature conservation and environmentally friendly disposition. Other options include mixing cremains into paint and having one's loved one painted as a memorial painting, melting the ashes into glass and turning them into a glass memorial sculpture, placing the ashes into vinyl to be made into vinyl records, and turning the ashes into carbon to be made into lab-made diamonds and wearable jewelry. Some have even mixed cremains into tattoo ink and had their loved ones tattooed onto their bodies. Cremains allow for a variety of creative disposition methods that are highly individualized, and their divisible nature permits people to elect to do different things with their portion of the remains.

Now that I have addressed more traditional religious views impacting disposition choice, I will turn in the rest of this chapter to highlight some of the more interesting forms of corpse disposition. Some of these forms of disposition intersect rather easily with religious worldviews (aquamation, for example, should align rather nicely with traditional worldviews on cremation, while offering a more environmentally friendly option), while others (cryonics as one example) might seem completely at odds with religious understandings of death and the afterlife (if one never dies, it makes it difficult to make the case for a religious afterlife). But disposition can reveal important values of the living and paint a picture of the way in which the living hope their lives to be understood long after they are gone.

EXCARNATION

Excarnation, or the practice of removing bodily flesh from bones through natural means, with vultures or intentional putrefaction by exposure to the elements, is another disposal practice observed in some religions such as Zoroastrianism or Tibetan Buddhism. In Zoroastrianism, traditional circular structures known as **towers of silence**, or **dakhma**, were built—large funerary towers built of stone or brick, in which bodies were laid out by gender and given to vultures to be consumed, allowing for the quick and efficient disposal of corpses. Usually the towers were built on a hill, and the sides of the towers were higher than the middle, which allowed for corpses to be excarnated in privacy. In Zoroastrianism, it is believed that death is so polluting and defiling that it can contaminate even the elements of earth (through burial), fire (through cremation), and water (in sea burial). Thus, the dakhma was a way around the polluting effects of death and decomposition. Outlawed in Iran in the seventies, towers of silence continued to be found in both Mumbai and Karachi, although there seems to have been an issue with an unexpected reduction in vultures, which has led to the excarnation process taking far longer than expected, and resulting in distasteful smells for the communities in which the towers were built. Zoroastrianism is not the only religion to practice excarnation; in Tibetan Buddhism, **sky burial** is regularly practiced, and the entire corpse is laid out on the ground and given to vultures to eat. When only the bones remain, the bones are broken down, mixed with barley flower and yak butter, and then fed to crows. This makes sense in the frozen tundra of the Himalayas, where the ground is often frozen, and excarnation of a corpse by vultures would be far more expedient than trying to dispose of a body in the frozen earth.

AQUAMATION OR ALKALINE HYDROLISIS

Aquamation or **alkaline hydrolysis** (sometimes also known as resomation or water cremation; there doesn't seem to be a singular term for this form of disposal yet) is similar to cremation in that it reduces the body to ash remains, though rather than using flames, it utilizes a combination of hot water and potassium hydroxide to liquify the body, leaving only the bones behind. The water is then flushed into the sewage system and the bones pulverized (like cremation) to a fine ash, which are then given back to the loved ones of the deceased for disposal and/or memorialization. Not yet widely adopted or utilized, particularly outside of the United States, aquamation originated in 1995 as a way for American medical facilities to dispose of bodies donated to science. However, funeral homes didn't offer this technology until 2011, and some states offer aquamation only for animals, but not for humans. Aquamation is touted as a more environmentally friendly option than cremation since it involves zero greenhouse emissions and does not require fossil fuels and very little energy. Additionally, there are approximately 20% more ash remains than cremation, largely because the heat from cremation does burn some of the bones, while aquamation mostly leaves the bones intact. Hopefully, in time, aquamation will become more widely adopted since it is far more environmentally friendly and inexpensive (the costs are estimated to be around $2,000–$3,000) than many other current disposition options.

How Do You Want to be Disposed of Once You Die?

Did you know you can outline your disposal wishes before you die? Some funeral homes will even let you pre-pay and pre-plan your funeral. You can decide how you want to be disposed (natural burial, cremation, etc.) and you can even plan what songs you want played or what foods you would like served at your memorial. This also helps your family since they will know that they are honoring you in a way that was important to you. If you don't have a preference, talk to your loved ones and see what might be important to them to help them through your loss. The following guidelines might be helpful as you plan.

Disposal: How do you want to be disposed of and why? Explain in detail.
Service: You should include the following:

- Location (graveside, funeral home, church, outside, family home, etc.)
- Invitees (who do you want there?)
- Type of service (will you have a wake? will this be a celebration of life or a memorial service, etc.)
- The celebrant (who is leading the service?)

- What do you want said/done at the service (will people give speeches, show videos, etc.)?
- What will the reception be like? Will the reception be at the funeral home/church/your house, etc.?
- Will there be food? If so, what foods?
- What prayers or readings do you want?
- Will you have pallbearers or a procession?
- What music will you have? (include a brief playlist)
- Will you have flowers? What kind?

PROMESSION

Originally developed in Sweden and not yet legal in the United States, **promession** breaks down the corpse through freeze-drying and utilizes about one-third of the energy of cremation. First, the decedent is frozen to zero degrees Fahrenheit, and then the body is placed in liquid nitrogen where it is crystallized. After a couple of hours, the liquid nitrogen then evaporates into the atmosphere, so this process of disposition is much more environmentally friendly. Finally, the body undergoes a minute of ultrasonic vibration, reducing the remains into a powder which is then disposed of in a similar way to cremains. These promession remains can also be added to soil and composting, since the nitrogen can aid in plant growth. Since promession isn't widely practiced and isn't yet legal, it is difficult to find the costs for this form of disposition.

COMPOSTING

Composting is another form of body disposition not yet widely adopted, but far more environmentally friendly. In this form of disposal, the body undergoes a process of natural organic reduction, or human composting, by being placed in a bin with wood chips and straw, which is mixed with soil. Then, the soil is regularly turned as the body decomposition is accelerated through composting. The process takes about two months and the soil can then be returned to the loved ones of the deceased in order to fertilize the ground and grow a tribute tree (or anything else they desire to grow) or donated to an ecological restoration project. Currently, there is only one place in the United States where people can be composted (Washington state), but composting shows promise as a disposition model for the environmentally conscious. Composting is approximately $5,500 and most of the cost covers the materials and human labor required for actively composting a body. The cost is more expensive than cremation, but about one-third to half the cost of embalming and burying a body, so composting also shows promise as an alternative and affordable form of disposition.

GREEN BURIALS

Green burial, also known as **natural burial**, is a way of burying the dead in a way that minimizes environmental impact and aids in the good stewardship of natural resources while reducing carbon emissions. Green burial is similar to composting in its ultimate aims, but different in its method, in that green burial is generally direct burial of the corpse, and there is no active aiding in the process of decomposition. Many cemeteries have traditionally not utilized natural burial, because dirt often caves in as the body decomposes, leaving uneven grounds (which is why cemeteries often require funeral plots to have **burial vault liners**, or cement boxes in which the caskets will be placed). Green burial grounds require that all materials placed in the ground be biodegradable in order to conserve the environment. This means that not only are caskets made of wood or cardboard, but that bodies may not be embalmed if they are to be buried on natural burial grounds. There are currently around 166 natural burial cemeteries in the United States, and natural burial is increasing around the world as people become more environmentally conscious. It is important to note here that environmental impact is superseding the importance of aesthetics so valued in cemeteries in the last several hundred years.

BODY FARMS

Another lesser known form of body disposition are **body farms**. A body farm is a research facility where body decomposition can be studied in a variety of settings, and whose findings have greatly aided in the advancement of scientific research and forensic science. Today, there are seven body farms in the United States (the University of Tennessee, Western Carolina University, Texas State University, Sam Houston State University, Southern Illinois University, Colorado Mesa University, and the University of South Florida), each one strategically chosen for its weather and climate so that variations in body decomposition might be observed and understood. University of Tennessee anthropologist Dr. Bill Bass founded the first body farm in 1987, and since then body farms have been instrumental in aiding law enforcement in identifying the role of body decomposition and pinpointing the time and manner of death in events ranging from homicide, suicide, and even refugee deaths. Since the original body farm's founding, Australia founded a body farm in 2016, Canada established one in 2018, and there are currently plans to establish one in India. Body farms, as gruesome as some may think they sound, have made important contributions in advancing the field of forensic anthropology and in helping scientists to better understand how body decomposition works. People can choose to donate their bodies to body farms in order to aide in this important work.

CRYONICS AND TRANSHUMANISM: TECHNOLOGIES AND DEATH

Cryonics and transhumanism might challenge more traditional notions of death, but deserve to be mentioned here, since their fundamental aim is extending life and eliminating death. The first one, **cryonics**, is a technique in which people who are declared legally dead are cryo-preserved in liquid nitrogen in order to preserve the body and prevent physical decay in the hopes of scientifically resurrecting them in the future (for more on cryonics, see https://www.cryonics.org). **Transhumanism** is the idea that technology and scientific advancement can be used to circumvent human limitations such as sickness, suffering, and death itself. In many ways, technology has changed the definition and understanding of death (through "life support" for example), so the idea that as technology continues to develop and advance we will possibly be able to challenge death itself is not as far-fetched as it first may seem.

The faith placed in scientific technology is in some ways similar to the faith placed in religious worldviews by religious adherents, though the afterlife envisioned here is a technological and futuristic one. Some transhumanist organizations in the United States hold status as official religious organizations, and while not a theistic tradition, in many ways, transhumanists deal with religious questions—of theodicy, of meaning, and of afterlife.

CONCLUSION

With growing issues regarding land scarcity, inhibitive disposition costs, and environmental concerns, disposal choices are rapidly shifting to ways in which bodies can be disposed of in a way that families and friends can mourn their loved ones without negatively impacting the realm of the living. This area remains one to watch, and it will be interesting to see the ways in which afterlife imaginaries shift and transform according to the needs of the living. The Catholic Church, for example, shifted its official position on cremation in 2016 because of increasing utilization by Catholic adherents of cremation because of its low cost. The Vatican decided that while cremation could be officially sanctioned by the church, it remains important that Catholics not divide the ashes, and that they are buried on sanctified ground, rather than scattered. In this way, Catholics may now choose cremation as their disposition choice, as long as they inter them on sacred ground. Thus, the practical concerns of body disposal have impacted afterlife imaginaries and ultimately religious belief. In Chapter 4, we will more deeply examine various religious understandings of the afterlife.

NOTE

1 Portions of pages 33–38 come from my previously published chapter "Mapping religious beliefs through consumer death goods," from my book *The Routledge Handbook of Death and the Afterlife* (2018).

REFERENCES

All Muslim Association of America (AMAA). n.d. http://www.amaacemetery.org, last accessed May 1, 2022.

Barker, Kenneth L., Mark L. Strauss, Jeannine K. Brown, Craig L. Blomberg, and Michael Williams, eds. *NIV Study Bible*. Grand Rapids, MI: Zondervan, 2020.

Crazy Coffins. n.d. (http://www.crazycoffins.co.uk/, last accessed May 9, 2022.

Funeral Practices Committee of The Board of Rabbis of Southern California. n.d. "A Guide to Jewish Burial and Mourning Practices," https://www.boardofrabbis.org/files/Funeral_Practices_Guide.pdf, last accessed March 10, 2022; site inactive on August 22, 2022.

International Association of Jewish Genealogical Societies. n.d. International Jewish Cemetery Project. IAJGS International Jewish Cemetery Project. http://www.iajgsjewishcemeteryproject.org/united-states/index.html, last accessed May 12, 2022.

Lamm, Maurice. n.d. "Grave Visitations and Prayers in Judaism," Chabad.org. https://www.chabad.org/library/article_cdo/aid/281633/jewish/Grave-Visitations-and-Prayers-in-Judaism.htm, last accessed May 11, 2022.

Malek, Alia. 2006. For Muslim New Yorkers, Final Rites that Fit. The New York Times. January 8. http://www.nytimes.com/2006/01/08/nyregion/thecity/08burial.html?_r=0, last accessed April 20, 2022.

Muslim Funeral Services, Ltd. n.d. Ghusl and Burial Steps. Muslim Funeral Services, Ltd. http://www.mfs.asn.au/ghusl–burial-steps.html, last accessed April 22, 2022.

FURTHER READING

Bryant, Clifton D., ed. *Handbook of Death and Dying*. Vol. 1 and 2. Thousand Oaks, CA: Sage, 2003.

Though a couple of decades old, this handbook is a valuable and comprehensive resource for different cultural attitudes on death, dying, and disposal.

Cann et al. COVID Paper "Alternate & Creative Disposal Options," https://www.covidpaper.org/resources/alternateoptions

Many types of contemporary disposal options are listed in this paper, illustrating the many options available today.

Cryonics Institute Technology for Life. https://www.cryonics.org/about-us/faqs/

The Cryonics Institute has a great FAQ section for those interested in knowing more about cryonics and the ways in which it works.

Mitford, Jessica. *The American Way of Death Revisited*. New York: Alfred A.
    Knopf, 1998.

This revision of her 1963 classic study of the American funeral industry
remains the best analysis of the profit-driven nature of the death and disposal
business in the United States.

Parkes, Colin Murray, Pittu Laungani, and William Young, eds. *Death and
    Bereavement across Cultures*. London: Routledge, 2015.

This book is a great resource for the cross-comparison of views of death in
different cultures and religions. In many of these chapters, there are also men-
tions of burial practices, including a chapter written about secularization and
child death and bereavement.

GRIEF, BEREAVEMENT, AND MOURNING

THE STUDY OF GRIEF

Like the study of death, the history of the academic study of grief, bereavement, and mourning is almost as interesting as the theories themselves, and deserves a brief mention here in order to understand how the study of grief as a discipline initially emerged. Up until the twentieth century, infant mortality rates were fairly high and life expectancy was much lower. In the United Kingdom in 1850, for example, the average life expectancy was 42 for a man and 40 for a woman, and 25% of children died by the age of 5; in China, both men and women could expect to live until age 32, and 42% of children died before their fifth birthday. On a global scale, people were far more accustomed to living with death, grief, and mourning on a daily basis. As a result, mourning was also public. Some death scholars (Gorer,1955; Becker,1997; Ariès, 1982) argue that up until World War I, everyone mourned publicly, and that after World War I, people stopped expressing their grief in public ways and turned inward. As a result parents didn't talk about their grief, and children didn't learn about death as a part of everyday life, leaving them essentially unprepared regarding how to act and feel about death. This shift from public expression to private feeling created a space for the psychological idea of the "grief process," and the notion that grief is an individuated experience, rather than a socially shared one. Sociologist Tony Walter argues for a more nuanced reading of this shift, arguing that class, gender, and the importance/influence of taboo created various pressures that might have led to this interpretation. Regardless, however, it is important

DOI: 10.4324/9780429025075-4

to understand that along with the rise of psychology as a discipline in the late 1800s, this shift from understanding grief as a collective experience to a highly individuated private encounter with death has helped create an entire discipline, resulting in theories and processes that are now considered normative frameworks for grieving.

GRIEF, BEREAVEMENT, AND MOURNING

Grief is a reaction to the loss of a person, thing, or situation that is valued by a person. Grief can be experienced over any kind of loss, and is not limited only to death and dying, but also can be experienced in times of transition or even changes in circumstance. People grieve the loss of a job, a relationship, a friend moving away, or any kind of significant change in their life that forces one to readjust. Grief can be experienced for minor losses, big losses, and for animals and things. One does not only experience grief over the loss of a person that one loves. Grief can also be felt over the death of someone who has been distant, harmful, or abusive, and this can often feel confusing since one might simultaneously feel sad over the death, but perhaps relieved that the source of their suffering is no longer present. In these cases, often people feel sad because they are unable to confront their tormenter and might feel as though now they have to live without closure. Similarly, grief can be experienced over an imagined future—a miscarriage is often difficult because it is not merely the loss of a baby that one must confront, but the loss of an imagined future, and a changed landscape that now no longer exists. Finally, one can also feel **anticipatory grief**, or the grief that is felt before a loss, when one knows that another person or pet is going to die soon. Anticipatory grief can help prepare one for the loss that is coming and might feel strange for the griever because they are experiencing the realization of loss before it has even occurred.

While grief is the personal experience to a loss, **bereavement** is a term used to designate the time during which a person experiences their grief and describes the state of having experienced a loss. While grief is a reaction to loss, bereavement is a state of being in which a person finds themselves. **Bereavement leave** is the term used by workplaces to describe an amount of time given from work to manage the affairs of the deceased, plan the funeral, and/or mourn. With the exception of the United States, most countries offer federally mandated bereavement leave. In the United States, however, bereavement leave is left up to individual companies, and can range from a few hours (to attend a funeral) to a few days, depending on the relationship of the deceased to the griever.

Finally, **mourning** is the way in which grief is expressed in public. Mourning may involve particular rituals, practices, and or customs, but is usually a public expression of loss. These customs can range from wearing particular clothing to honor the deceased to eating particular foods, reciting particular prayers, following religious rituals, and remembering the dead on certain days of remembrance. Mourning rituals vary widely, and are heavily dependent on culture, religious context, local tradition, identity, and practice. In short, grief is essentially what a person feels and thinks on the inside in response to a loss, while mourning is what they do to honor and observe that loss in front of others.

THE PURPOSE OF GRIEF, BEREAVEMENT, AND MOURNING

Grief, bereavement, and mourning all serve an important function. First, they acknowledge the finality and fragility of life and the awareness that all beings who live will also one day die. In this way, life is like a book, and the purpose of grief is to make sense of the book—to read it, understand it, and digest it. Bereavement might be like a book club that meets regularly to understand and interpret the book, and mourning might function like a library, creating a decimal system to organize and order the books on shelves to create order and make sense of the various lives and deaths that we encounter. In this way, they all work together, and while you don't *need* a book club or a library to read and understand a book, they can help bring new meaning and make sense of the book in ways we cannot always do on our own. Studies have shown that we must grieve—we must learn somehow to grapple with the meaning of death and the existential questions that death brings with it—in order to live well. Grief is painful and can be quite difficult, but it is also an essential part of the human condition—regardless of culture, religion, identity, or country. So now, we turn to some of the studies on grief and the theories surrounding it.

GRIEF THEORY

Grief theory is the study of how humans remember and mourn the dead, while making sense of the loss in their lives. As a result, many different theories regarding grief have emerged—with various and often incorrect—assumptions emerging around the topic. Unfortunately some of the most egregious thinkers on the topic remain some of the most well-known, causing much consternation to the average person over whether their feelings of loss are "normal." Sigmund Freud's book *Mourning and Melancholia* (1917) offered one of the first in-depth analyses of grief, arguing that while mourning might be normal, the melancholy that lingered might be viewed as abnormal or pathological. Because grief is normal and a part of life, Freud's work has not borne the test of time and his essential theories regarding grief have largely been debunked. There are cases in which grief might be labeled as **complicated grief** (grief that tends to last a longer than average period of time and that keeps one in an ongoing heightened state of mourning), but most often complicated grief results from a traumatic death such as the death of a child, a homicide, or an unexpected death, or because there may have been some particularly painful dynamics between the living and the deceased that were never resolved, and the living remains in a state of limbo as a result.

Elisabeth Kübler-Ross is another theorist who has helped make death, dying, and grief particularly visible, but whose scholarship has been largely misunderstood and misapplied to grief work. Kübler-Ross' (1981) stages of grief were initially formulated as stages of the dying process of a dying person, not a grieving one. These stages include the five stages that a dying patient passes through as they come to acknowledge that their death is impending (they are denial, anger, bargaining, depression, and acceptance). However, not only have these stages been misapplied from dying to grief, they are often interpreted as five steps that one must undertake to be considered successful in the grieving process. Unfortunately, these stages still remain heavily visible in the public realm, and many professionals who work with grieving families continue to wrongly believe that these stages are formative and important indicators of grief success.

Somewhat similar to Kübler-Ross, clinical psychologist **Therese Rando**'s tasks of mourning (Rando, 1984) view grief as a shift from loss recognition to a readjustment to a new world without the deceased. Therese Rando describes what she calls the **6 Rs of healthy grief**: (1) Recognize the loss, (2) React to the loss, (3) Recollect and Re-Experience the lost relationship, (4) Relinquish, and put the loss behind you, (5) Readjust, and (6) Reinvest. According to Rando, one moves through three different stages as the person adjusts to the loss of their loved one. They move gradually from a reactive avoidance to the death to a time of confronting the death and making sense of it, to finally figuring out one's place in the world without the deceased. While these six Rs might look similar to Kübler-Ross' stages, these are far more complex, and tailored to a grieving person. Multiple studies have revealed, though, that generally, **stage-based models** are not only unhealthy, but in some instances, actually counter-indicative to healthy grieving.

More commonly accepted and utilized, **Erich Lindemann**'s (1979) model of **grief work** or **William Worden**'s (1996) **tasks of mourning** offer somewhat better alternatives to stage-based theories. Lindemann (1979) argued that there were three primary tasks of grief: (1) The emancipation of bondage from the deceased, (2) the readjustment to a new environment without the deceased, and (3) the formation of new relationships. While Lindemann's model is more helpful than a stage-based model, it still takes its cues from the Protestant notion that the dead no longer occupy space in the living world, in contrast to many other religious worldviews that view the dead as occupying the world of the living in an altered state, or occasionally interacting with the living on specific religious holidays. Conversely, William Worden's theory of grief allows for an "enduring connection with the deceased." His tasks of mourning are (1) to accept the reality of the loss, (2) to work through the pain of grief, (3) to adjust to an environment in which the deceased is missing, and (4) to find an enduring connection with the deceased while embarking on a new life (Worden, 2009). Worden's tasks of mourning can work in a variety of cultural and religious interpretation since the connection with the deceased can either be through memory and sense-making or a form of continuing bonds in which the deceased regularly revisits the world of the living. If there are any drawbacks to Worden's theory, it is that it views grief as work to "get through," rather than grief to "live with." The key similarity of all of these grief theories is that they assume a linear and progressive timeline for grief, which views grief as work or tasks to be undertaken by the bereaved.

GOOD GRIEF THEORIES

Grief impacts people psychologically/emotionally, behaviorally, cognitively, physically, and socially, impacting individuals, families, and society. Good grief therapies generally encourage someone to learn how to live with the grief, to incorporate the grief into their daily life, and share that grief with others, knowing that the way this grief feels and looks will shift on a regular basis. **Margaret Stroebe** and **Henk Schut**'s **dual-process model** of grief suggests that the bereaved person oscillates between a **loss orientation** and a **restoration orientation** model of coping, in which a person may feel the loss of their loved one keenly, followed by periods in which they feel okay again, but the process continually shifts, and sometimes one feels both ways at once (see Schut and Stroebe's original 1999 article and Schut and Strobe's 2010 review). The dual process model recognizes the ongoing unpredictability of grief and acknowledges that the living may continue to have a relationship with the deceased. Along with Continuing Bonds theory and Narrative Grief Therapy, both discussed below, Stroebe and Schut's dual-process model may be one of the more optimal grief theories today, because it allows for universal applicability in spite of cultural and religious variation, while also advocating for the incorporation of grief and grief experience into everyday life.

Expanding on the importance of incorporating grief into everyday experience, **Continuing Bonds Theory** argues that grief may in fact be a life-long process—one that may not ever be completed or finished—and validates continuing a new and ongoing relationship with the deceased. Relationships with the dead are not static ones, but changing and valuable ones that will continue to develop as we move through life. **Klass, Silverman, and Nickman's** (1996) theory of "continuing bonds" describes what many around the world consider to be caring for the dead, and is a dominant grief paradigm in the non-Western world. No longer viewed as part of a maladaptive grieving process, Klass, Nickman, and Silverman view the ongoing attachment to the deceased as healthy and even expected. In short, this "model of grieving … focuses on the complexity of human relationships and the ways in which people remain connected to each other in life and in death" (Bowlby, 1980, p. 22). While Continuing Bonds Theory has seen wide acceptance in the United Kingdom and in Europe, it has not yet been broadly promoted in the United States, even though in some ways, it is one of the more pluralistic and ecumenical grief theories in the toolbox. As Klass writes in his 2014 article, "Grief, consolation, and religions: A conceptual framework," "We noted that the most common consolation in the histories of religions comes within continuing bonds with the dead, and we showed the difficulty [that] contemporary bereaved people have in a culture that does not include continuing bonds in its narrative." Continuing Bonds Theory emerged from Klass' fieldwork in Japan when he found that those cultures that embed the notion of continuing bonds within their religious worldviews seem to have the most successful integration of grief into their everyday lives. For Klass, offering a different framework for thinking about and relating to the dead within a heavily secular and Protestant culture, offers a chance for people to re-member the dead and re-situate themselves into the world of the living.

Finally, **Robert Neimeyer**'s **Narrative Grief Therapy** utilizes a variety of narrative and artistic tools to encourage grievers to reconstruct meaning in a world without their loved ones (Neimeyer, 1999, 2001). Being able to name one's feelings, find words to express our loss, and engage in artistic expression to convey our emptiness is no small thing in a world that has suddenly shifted, and in which the absence of another is a huge vacuum that others may not necessarily share. For Neimeyer, grieving "requires us to reconstruct a world that again 'makes sense,' that restores a semblance of meaning, direction, and interpretability to a life that is forever transformed" (Neimeyer, 2006, p. 92). Neimeyer's meaning-making can take many forms in grief—whether ritual, narrative, art, or community. The important part is that the world is built anew—with a recognition of loss and all the space that loss gives to create. While some grief theories are more universally applicable to different cultures and religions than others, these grief theories all share the same aim: They encourage us to grieve and validate the constant shifting one feels after a loss. Grief is a lifelong process that one learns to incorporate into one's life, and is a part of the natural world as all things that live will one day also come to die.

One final note must be made here regarding the importance of grief theory to the contemporary medical system—particularly in the United States, where grief is categorized as a mental illness in order for the costs of counseling to be covered by insurance. Bereavement is normal and it is not generally classified as a disease. In order for costs to be covered by medical insurance, however, the **DSM-5** (the Diagnostic and Statistical Manual of Mental Disorders), which is the insurance coding manual that doctors use to bill insurance providers for their services, classifies bereavement as a medical disorder if the grief lasts longer than two weeks and/or causes depressive symptoms. The intent of this was good—it allows for patients to have their grief counseling costs to be covered by insurance. The outcome of this has been a bit more complicated, as patients often feel as though they are being told they should not experience grief for more than two weeks, or that their grief should not cause them depressive symptoms. In short, some critics feel that grief has become medicalized or pathologized as a result of trying to create a way for doctors to be able to utilize billing codes that insurance will reimburse.

Your Grief

Grief is not just for when people die. We grieve loss and change too. For example, many people lost their jobs during the pandemic, or maybe they realized that the job was no longer a good fit for their work-life balance, or their values. Some people got a divorce. Others moved. Some had a dear pet die. These are all losses worthy of being grieved over. Sometimes we don't realize we are grieving because we haven't taken the time to reflect on how we are doing, or we think that in comparison to others, our loss isn't worthy. ALL grief is valid.

Here are some tips that might help:

- *Identify grief*: Have you been angry lately or short-tempered and haven't known why? This might be because you are sad, and not sure where to put those feelings. It might be helpful to write down your feelings so that they begin to untangle.
- *Embrace the feelings and validate them*: You might not want to feel the pain, but you can only live with grief by first validating it, and experiencing it.
- *Share the feelings*: Identify a support system that will validate your feelings of loss. If you don't have one, find one. There are many online groups and you can retain anonymity if that is important to you. Go to therapy. Write your feelings and thoughts in a journal.
- *Exercise*: This may sound strange but grief lives in the body even if you don't want to face it. Exercise helps create natural endorphins that will make you feel more equipped to deal with grief.
- *Make room for your grief*: Allow room for your grief both literally and figuratively. If someone you loved or a pet you cared for died recently, make space for them in a physical and symbolic way. Leave a place for Dad at the table, put your pet's picture on your mantle along with his favorite snack. Doing this shows you that you haven't forgotten them and lets you honor them in a meaningful way.

THE SOCIOLOGICAL STUDY OF GRIEF

While grief theory has been fundamental to the field of psychology, and is largely seen as the purview of medicine, more scholars are now viewing the importance of grief as a social phenomenon that should be studied at the societal level. As Nina Jakoby (2012) writes, "The concept of normal grief is an ideal that tells us how to grieve. It is a specific Western cultural model of grief that does not correspond to reality and everyday experiences of loss. It is a social and cultural construction maintained by science, especially psychiatrics and health professionals." Thus, the sociology of grief offers an important counter-narrative to the traditional medical examination of grief. Grief is not merely experienced at the individual level, and there are deaths that affect society at large, which people are forced to reckon with as a society. **Mass casualty** events, like school shootings, wars, pandemics, or famines, have helped to increase the interest in examining the topic of grief and its impact at a broader societal level. **Popular memorialization**, or the communal grief expressed by groups of people over the deaths of cultural icons, also reveals a move toward grief expression that moves beyond individuals. (I should note here that communal grief differs from mourning in that mourning is the commonly expressed way of expressing grief, whereas **communal grief** is a group of people experiencing grief over a death, but perhaps in different and varying ways, with no universal or set expression of mourning).

This has also led to the sociological examination of grief and its impact on society. Sociological studies of grief impact the exchange between grief and shifts in society, and can include studies such as:

- Changes in status as a result of death
- The impact of gender roles and expectations in the expression of grief
- Shifts in power dynamics as a result of death, and the ways in which death and grief contribute to, reinforce, or detract from power
- Hospitality exchanges between the living and the dead, and/or the living and the living (e.g., funeral feasts might address food insecurity while also reinforcing status)
- An examination of social resources and support around both the living and the dead
- An emphasis of belonging and identity through rituals for the dead
- Coping styles as indicative of wealth and class
- An examination of marginal identity through a politics of exclusion (e.g., who gets to mourn and for whom)

While not exhaustive, these ways of examining grief reveal that it is important to move beyond the more medicalized model of grief as experienced only by an individual, and instead focus on the ways in which grief can impact and affect social groups and societies.

In Chapter 5, we will briefly examine the ways in which religion interprets and ritualizes bereavement, examining the aspects of grief from various religious perspectives. As you read about these bereavement customs from various religious perspectives, think about ways in which these religious traditions may either be useful for developing coping skills in the grieving process, or whether the religious worldview may be maladaptive and create barriers for healthy grieving in light of the many grief theories you have learned about in the chapter.

REFERENCES

Ariès, Philippe. *The Hour of our Death*. New York: Vintage, 1982.

Becker, Ernest. *The Denial of Death*. New York: Simon and Schuster, 1997.

Bowlby, John. *Attachment and Loss: Vol. 3: LOSS*. London: Hogarth Press and the Institute of Psycho-Analysis, 1980.

Freud, Sigmund. "Mourning and melancholia." *Standard Edition*14, no. 239 (1917): 1957–1961.

Gorer, Geoffrey. "The pornography of death." *Encounter* 5, no. 4 (1955): 49–52.

Jakoby, Nina R. "Grief as a social emotion: Theoretical perspectives." *Death Studies* 36, no. 8 (2012): 679–711.

Klass, Dennis, Phyllis R. Silverman, and Steven L. Nickman, eds. *Continuing Bonds: New Understandings of Grief*. Milton Park, UK: Taylor & Francis, 1996.

Kübler-Ross, Elisabeth. *Living with Death and Dying* New York: Macmillan, 1981.

Lindemann, Erich. *Beyond Grief: Studies in Crisis Intervention* New York: Aronson, 1979.

Neimeyer, Robert A. "Narrative strategies in grief therapy." *Journal of Constructivist Psychology* 12, no. 1 (1999): 65–85.

Neimeyer, Robert A. "Reauthoring life narratives: Grief therapy as meaning reconstruction." *The Israel Journal of Psychiatry and Related Sciences* 38, no. 3/4 (2001): 171–183.

Neimeyer, Robert A. *Lessons of Loss: A Guide to Coping*. Memphis, TN: Center for the Study of Loss and Transition, 2006.

Rando, Therese A. *Grief, Dying, and Death: Clinical Interventions for Caregivers*. Champaign, IL: Research Press Company, 1984.

Schut, Margaret and Henk Stroebe. "The dual process model of coping with bereavement: Rationale and description." *Death Studies* 23, no. 3 (1999): 197–224.

Stroebe, Margaret, and Henk Schut. "The dual process model of coping with bereavement: A decade on." *OMEGA-Journal of Death and Dying* 61, no. 4 (2010): 273–289).

Worden, J. William. "Tasks and mediators of mourning: A guideline for the mental health practitioner." *In Session: Psychotherapy in Practice: Psychotherapy in Practice* 2, no. 4 (1996): 73–80.

Worden, J. William. *Grief Counseling and Grief Therapy: a Handbook for the Mental Health Practitioner* 4th ed. New York, NY: Springer Pub. Co., 2009.

FOR FURTHER READING

Grief and Religion

Hass, Jeffrey K., and Tony Walter. "Parental grief in three societies: Networks and religion as social supports in mourning." *OMEGA-Journal of Death and Dying* 54, no. 3 (2007): 179–198.

While this qualitative study of different parental responses to infant death is specifically geared to infant loss, the study highlights the importance of structural and cultural factors and their impact on grief overall.

Lee, Sherman A., Laurin B. Roberts, and Jeffrey A. Gibbons. "When religion makes grief worse: Negative religious coping as associated with maladaptive emotional responding patterns." *Mental Health, Religion and Culture* 16, no. 3 (2013): 291–305.

This article highlights the ways in which negative religious coping highlighted dysfunctional grief patterns and prolonged recovery.

Grief Theory

Granek, L. "Grief as pathology: The evolution of grief theory in psychology from Freud to the present." *History of Psychology* 13, no. 1 (2010): 46–73. https://doi.org/10.1037/a0016991

This article is a great resource for following the progression of Grief theory in the last hundred years through 2010.

Klass, Dennis. "Grief, consolation, and religions: A conceptual framework." *OMEGA-Journal of Death and Dying* 69, no. 1 (2014): 1–18.

This article seeks to define grief more broadly in order to include the inner-subjective aspects which both include and are shaped by exterior culture and religion.

Maciejewski, Paul K., Baohui Zhang, Susan D. Block, and Holly G. Prigerson. "An empirical examination of the stage theory of grief." *Jama* 297, no. 7 (2007): 716–723. https://jamanetwork.com/journals/jama/articlepdf/205661/joc70007_716_723.pdf

This study was established to "examine the relative magnitudes and patterns of change over time post-loss for consistency with the stage theory of grief." Essentially, it examines the efficacy of stage theory of grief widely taught, but which had never been empirically studied, and found variations among type of loss (e.g., natural vs. traumatic), and argued for adjustments to stage–based theories.

Sociology of Grief

Jakoby, Nina R. "Grief as a social emotion: Theoretical perspectives." *Death studies* 36, no. 8 (2012): 679–711.

Jokoby's article argues for the importance of examining grief at a social level, moving beyond medical and psychological models of grief to a sociological one, because grief can have societal implications and impacts.

Walter, Tony. "Modern death: taboo or not taboo?" *Sociology* 25, no. 2 (1991): 293–310.

This is a solid and thorough examination of the move from collective grief to private grief and the study of death in general through a historical disciplinary lens.

Walter, Tony. "A sociology of grief." *Mortality* 3, no. 1 (1998): 83–87.

Walter's article gives a brief and succinct overview of the development of the field of grief from a sociological perspective.

MOURNING AND BEREAVEMENT FROM A RELIGIOUS PERSPECTIVE

INTRODUCTION

Many people rely on religious beliefs to help them in the grieving process. Religion can often be helpful in providing comfort
to the living as they work to process loss, and beliefs in an afterlife can frequently aid in an imagined existence following a death.
Religious communities and rituals can provide a sort of grammar
of mourning as one works to process a life without the deceased,
and traditional mourning rites can help to provide structure, offer
sense-meaning, and give community and support in the difficult
time following a death. Not all religious approaches to mourning, however, are helpful, and sometimes people will find that they
question their religion and sense of religious belonging as they
confront new existential questions regarding living and dying.
This is entirely normal, as people have varying responses to death,
and often, particularly in contemporary society, we are not given
much training in how to respond to, or think about, death. In this
way, some religious responses may be maladaptive and impede grief
recovery. The role of religion in one's mourning will be affected by
many variables including personal belief, level of integration of an
individual within a religion, the experiences of religious practitioners with death, dying, and grief, support systems surrounding death
and grief, and to some extent, afterlife beliefs themselves. Afterlife
imaginaries will inform, affect, and alter the grief journey, and in
some ways may contribute to successful or maladaptive grief processes. For example, religions that provide a way for the grieving to
have continuing bonds with the deceased through regular care for

DOI: 10.4324/9780429025075-5

the dead may give the living a way to integrate the dead into their daily lives and allow the grieving person to move forward *with* the dead in a new way. Some religions, though, emphasize the absence of the dead, and do not encourage (and often do not permit) a relationship with the deceased, which may make the absence more traumatic and the grief journey more difficult.

JEWISH MOURNING TRADITIONS

In Judaism, it is customary to observe a mourning period, known as **shiva**, following the death of a loved one. Shiva comes from the Hebrew word seven and correlates to the expected seven-day mourning period for all Jewish mourners. During this time, mourners are expected to withdraw from all social activities, to perform no tasks that might be associated with work (with two exceptions—the possibility of extreme financial hardship and if one's occupation involves saving others' lives, such as a doctor or a nurse), and to devote themselves solely to the task of grieving. Mourners are not supposed to leave their house during this period, except to observe **Shabbat**, the Sabbath, or the day of rest, at the synagogue. The custom of observing shiva has its basis in the passage of Genesis 50:1-14, in which Joseph mourns the death of his father Jacob, or Israel, for seven days. The exceptions to observing the full seven-day period are the Jewish high holy days of Rosh Hashanah, Yom Kippur, Sukkot, Passover, and Shavuot. If one of these holy days occurs during a shiva, then the Jewish holiday takes precedence, and the rest of the shiva is cancelled. The reason for this is similar to the reason the bereaved still observe shabbat, the holy day of rest. God's worship takes precedence over bereavement. Thus, if a holiday occurs before a shiva has been completed, the holy day(s) take precedence. For this reason, it is also expected that during sabbath services, no public mourning may occur, as one is expected to focus solely on God.

Traditionally, while observing shiva, a candle is lit upon one's return from the funeral and burial of the deceased (or upon hearing of the death) that burns for the entire seven-day period. The candle symbolizes the bond between the deceased and the mourners, with the flame serving as a metaphor for the soul of the deceased. The candle remains lit during the entire period, even throughout the sabbath, and if the death occurred during a Jewish high holy day, then even though the burial and shiva may not occur immediately, the candle is still lit and kept lit for the holiday and the shiva period. One exception, however, is that during the celebration of the holiday, the candle should not be kept in the dining room but in a more private place, since the focus should remain on God's holiday. A prayer is spoken at the lighting of the candle and marks the beginning and end of the *shiva* mourning period. During shiva one is expected to forgo many of life's daily pleasures and mundane tasks. Bathing and grooming (particularly for pleasure) are given up, women usually wear no makeup, men give up shaving, and mirrors are covered during the duration of the mourning period so that one focuses inward and not on one's appearance. Jewish law also states that worship services may not be held where one can see a reflection of oneself, and since worship services are held in the home of the deceased, mirrors need to be covered in order for the prayer to occur. It is customary that one does not work during shiva, but when this is not possible, a minimum of three days in mourning is expected. Those observing shiva are traditionally expected to be humble and sit on low stools or chairs, but in reality this aspect of shiva is not always strictly observed, even though many mourners may remove the cushions from their sofas and chairs in order to sit on hard surfaces. All of these customs— covering mirrors, refraining from food preparation, and partaking in daily tasks or pleasures—are meant to remind the mourner of the absence of the deceased and to allow the bereaved to focus nearly exclusively on her loss.

It is considered a gift to participate in shiva, and there are several expectations placed upon the greater Jewish community surrounding the bereaved. One of these expectations includes the bringing of food to the house of the deceased. Because Jews observing shiva are neither allowed nor expected to prepare meals and may not serve those who come to visit, it becomes the task of the community to ensure that the bereaved are well fed and cared for. Thus, it is considered a blessing to prepare food for the bereaved, bring it to their home, and then serve them. Flowers are not an appropriate gift to a Jewish home, as they are not considered humble, but rather ostentatious and unnecessary. For this reason, most Jews prefer that a donation be made in honor of the deceased in order to honor their memory, and most Jews will have a preferred charity to which the grieving may give a charitable donation. This is considered a blessing to the deceased, as the deceased can never repay the gift given in their name.

Traditional Jewish custom dictates that mourners rip their clothing when someone close to them dies. Sometimes this custom is maintained today, but more often the ripped clothing is now replaced with a **keriah** ribbon that symbolizes the clothing. The ripping of the keriah is meant to symbolize the breaking of one's heart at the loss of a loved one. The ribbon (or ripped clothing) is then worn during the entire initial mourning period of seven days, or shiva. For those mourning the loss of one's parents, the keriah is worn over one's heart on the left side, and when mourning the loss of one's spouse, children, and/or siblings, it is worn over the right side.

The first meal following a funeral, the **seudat havra'ah**, is served at the home of the deceased upon returning from the cemetery and is usually provided by the family, friends, and synagogue of the bereaved. Among other foods served are things that are round in shape, symbolizing the cycle of life, such as hard-boiled eggs, bagels, round pasta, and round cakes. These are eaten to remind the grievers that death is only one part of life. This meal marks the official beginning of sitting shiva, the intense seven-day mourning period. In Jewish custom, it takes ten adults to form a **minyan**, or a quorum—the minimum number required to hold a public prayer service. This number is meant to remind Jews that although they may individually hold much power or prosperity, it is only when they form a group of ten or more that they can form a Jewish community with the power to hold a prayer service. It is said that this reinforces both humility and the importance of community in Judaism. Because it takes ten Jewish adults to hold a **shiva minyan**, or a prayer service for the dead, the act of visiting and participating in a shiva is considered to be another good deed in Judaism.

MUSLIM MOURNING TRADITIONS

Like Judaism, in Islam, the community plays an important role in providing support to those in mourning. Attending a funeral is considered to be meritorious, and Muslims are encouraged to attend funerals, whether they knew the deceased or not, because it demonstrates respect and care. Following a death, the initial bereavement period lasts three days, during which family members are encouraged to remain in the home in prayer. Widows, however, are expected to be in mourning for an extended period lasting four lunar months and ten days. During this time, the community helps care for the widow's needs so that she can focus on her mourning, and she is generally encouraged to stay home except for necessary medical appointments or essential business transactions. In more traditional Muslim cultures, loud or excessive weeping is discouraged. Since when and how one dies is considered to be part of God's plan, one is generally expected to accept the death as much as it might make one sad. In more patriarchal cultures, women are discouraged at the graveside funeral, but may visit once the body is interred. This is largely dependent on a cultural interpretation of Islam, though, and is not a universal proscription.

Simple clothes are worn, preferably all black, and no makeup or jewelry is permitted during this time. As with funeral attendance, it is generally considered a blessing to say prayers on behalf of the deceased, and for this reason, it is customary for extended family and friends to stop by the house of the bereaved to sit with those who are in mourning, and to extend care through shared presence. Also during this time, it is considered meritorious to visit the bereaved and make or bring food for them during the three days of mourning so that the family and friends of the deceased may center their attention and focus exclusively on mourning. In fact, it is not allowed for the bereaved family to cook or make food for those visiting them, since they are in mourning, so it is expected that visitors will attend to any food preparations at this time. The foods eaten and offered in this time vary culturally, but should adhere to **halal** dietary customs. Meaning "lawful" or "permitted," halal food—like kosher food in Judaism—is food that has been prepared in a humane and sanitary way according to Islamic law, including a proscription against pork, alcohol, and foods containing rennet or gelatin, etc. While food traditions at Muslim funerals vary across cultures (Moroccans often serve couscous dishes, while Persians serve rice pudding and halvah), the dishes are usually meant to serve a multitude of people over a few days.

HINDU MOURNING TRADITIONS

In Hinduism, the visitation and cremation occur quite quickly—usually within twenty-four hours—so the community comes together in the mourning period afterward to help the bereaved manage their grief. During the traditional mourning period (ten days for the initial mourning period, and a year for immediate family of the deceased), the family is considered to be ritually impure, and should not visit sacred sites, such as temples or family shrines. After the tenth day, between the eleventh and thirty-first day, depending on caste traditions, a **shraddha** ceremony is held in order to pay homage to the deceased. The shraddha is a memorial ceremony that usually consists of gift giving and feasting, and can last from days to weeks depending on who died and the means of the family holding the shraddha. It is commonly believed that whatever is given away during a shraddha will eventually find its way to the dead. The shraddha's hospitality exchanges reveal a world of interdependence between the living and the dead, as well as the family of the deceased and the broader community. The shraddha is hosted by a male descendant of the deceased, and as in China, this in part explains the importance of having children in Hindu culture—particularly male children who can perform the ceremony. If there is no male descendent, then the closest male relative takes this role upon themselves; this could be a grandson, nephew, or a cousin—the important thing is that the officiant is male. After the primary mourning period, the shraddha will be performed on a monthly basis for the first year, and then after the first year has passed, should be observed on an annual basis on the anniversary of the death. The observance of the shraddha is expected to occur for three generations, until the deceased becomes a familial ancestor, and individual memorialization is no longer considered necessary.

SIKH MOURNING TRADITIONS

Like Hinduism, Sikhs also prefer to cremate their dead, and generally only close friends and family are encouraged to attend the cremation, though the larger community may attend the funeral. Overt forms of grieving are discouraged since Sikhs believe that death allows for a return to Waheguru, and that the deceased body is only a shell of the person that was there before. Usually before a cremation, it is customary to have a short funeral at the temple or the funeral home, and the funeral itself lasts about an hour. A Sikh funeral consists of three core elements: A congregational community prayer read at the start of ceremonies, the **Japji,** which is the first verse of the Sikh holy book, and the Kirtan Sohila, the nighttime prayer, usually recited every evening before one goes to sleep. The congregants wear white (like much of Asia, white is the traditional color of mourning) and cover their heads.

Following the funeral service, the deceased is usually accompanied from the Gurudwara or funeral home to the site of cremation. Hymns and prayers are sung while accompanying the body, and once the body is laid on top of the cremation pyre, the eldest son is usually responsible for lighting the pyre (or if in an industrial cremation complex, pushing the button) to start the cremation process. During the process, the Kirtan Sohila (or nighttime prayers) are recited. Once the body is fully cremated, all of the ashes are either released in water or buried in the ground and the ground leveled. In Sikhism, it is strictly forbidden to erect a monument in honor of the dead and no marking of the remains are permitted. After the cremation, the congregation will usually gather to read the **Guru Granth Sahib**, the central text of Sikhism which is read in its entirety in forty-eight hours as a way to bring blessings, either at the home of the deceased or at the local temple. During the reading, the traditional sweet desert, **karhah prashad**, will be distributed. Made of flour, butter, sugar, and wheat, the karhah prashad is a sacred food, usually given as a sign of hospitality in Sikh ceremonies. Generally, the prayers should last no more than ten days and they are read by members of the household of the deceased, as a way to remember and honor the deceased. The purpose of the scripture reading is meant to be viewed as a way to remind the community of God, and Waheguru's love and purpose, even in death and sadness.

BUDDHIST MOURNING TRADITIONS

Within the three schools of Buddhism—Theravada, Mahayana, and Vajrayana—there are many sects of Buddhism, and cultural interpretations and understandings of Buddhist mourning rituals vary across context, but there are some universal practices. Generally, it is believed that at death the soul departs the body, and is then reborn in another life. Families often hold funerals on either the third, fifth, or seventh day following a death. In Asia, odd numbers are considered particularly fortuitous since they denote "becoming" and thus funerals are usually held on an odd day in order to increase good fortune. In preparation for a Buddhist funeral, the body is first washed, and then laid out in a wooden coffin, and in some countries—like Japan—it is important that the corpse's head points north, since it is believed that this was the direction that the Buddha faced when he died. In actuality, the practice of placing the corpse's head north may come from Hinduism, in which it is commonly believed that the soul leaves the body from the head and moves northward, facilitating easy rebirth. Usually the family of the deceased will stay with the deceased until their funeral, sometimes setting up tables and providing food and drink for those who come to pay their respects before the cremation or burial. In South Korea, for example, it is customary for the funeral and wake to last three days, with many people coming to pay their respects to the dead, share a meal together, offer monetary gifts, and pay their condolences before the final disposition. In almost all Buddhist funerals, attendees are expected to help offset the funeral costs with money—usually a socially set amount that is placed in an envelope and recorded in an attendance register at the entrance to the funeral hall. In Japan, China, Korea, and Thailand, for example, it is customary to give money to the family to offset funeral expenses. The funeral itself is usually short—lasting anywhere from an hour to an hour and a half, and consisting of sutra chanting, prayers, and funerary chants. The third, seventh, forty-ninth, and hundredth day following the death of a person are particularly significant, and the immediate mourning time is forty-nine days, or seven weeks of seven days, since many Buddhists believe that a soul is reborn on the forty-ninth day following a death. Prayers for the dead are recited during this forty-nine-day mourning period in order to help the deceased as they journey through their afterlife toward their next rebirth. These prayers help the dead, while giving the living something they can "do" to help aid the deceased.

CHINESE MOURNING TRADITIONS

In China, there are elaborate mourning traditions that differ from region to region (and have varied even more as diasporic Chinese communities have migrated around the world), but there are a few notable features that are almost universally practiced. The first is the notification of death through publicly sanctioned grief and wailing. The second is the wearing of mourning clothing and/ or armbands (discussed in more detail below). Third, there is the washing of the corpse and the offering of food and other goods needed by the dead in the afterlife (see box). Fourth, there is a transfer of the spirit of the deceased to a memorial tablet, which then functions as a material stand-in for the deceased in the family home. Finally, there is the playing of music and a formal procession for both the body and spirit tablet, followed by a funeral feast, marking the end of the funeral.

Following a person's death, the mirrors in the home of the deceased are removed or turned around, particularly if a wake is held in a home. Sometimes, people will also place a mirror on their front door to scare away the deceased just in case s/he decides to return as a ghost to visit the living. Since white is the color of mourning in China, a white cloth is placed across the main entrance of the house to mark the house as one in mourning. Sometimes a gong is also placed at the entrance of the doorway—on the left of the doorway for the death of a man and on the right for the death of a woman. Those in mourning traditionally wear white clothing, although now it has become more common and acceptable to wear dark somber clothes as well. Red (and other bright cheery colors such as pink) are not worn to funerals, as red symbolizes happiness, and is frequently worn at weddings. Mourners will wear armbands (males on their left arm; females on their right arm) when they are in mourning to indicate to others that they are grieving over a death. Depending on local tradition, the armbands are sometimes in particular colors to denote status and relationship to the deceased. Many people will wear these armbands for the first hundred days of mourning as a way to show respect to the deceased; the armband has the added benefit of letting the broader community know that a person is in mourning. Also, if someone close has died, it is considered unlucky in Chinese culture for that person to attend a more fortuitous occasion, as they might bring "bad luck" to the occasion. Thus, if a colleague's father recently died, she would not be expected (or even invited) to attend a wedding as the polluting effects of the death might migrate to the more happy wedding. This might seem harsh to someone unfamiliar with Chinese culture, but the release from the expectation to participate in something "happy" after a loss can also be viewed as a deeply communal act in which the community cares for those who are mourning. Similarly, it is customary in Chinese culture for funeral attendees to bring an envelope full of money in an odd amount (rather than even) to both help offset the costs of the funeral and to bring good luck to the dead. This has the functional purpose of helping the family with the various costs associated with making disposition arrangements. The custom of bringing money to help offset the costs of the funeral can be found across Asia in other Confucian cultures as well.

Last, it is customary to offer food and wine at a funeral, and the funeral feast has symbolic foods that are meant to comfort the spirit of the deceased as they embark on their journey to the underworld. Usually, the funeral feast includes fruit offerings placed in small towers, with colors symbolizing the Daoist elements and the five directions: Green is for east; yellow for the center; red is for south; white is for west; and black is for north. The five colors signify the various directions, and symbolically guide the deceased on their journey. Other traditional funeral foods are uncooked rice, twice-cooked pork, and chicken. All of these foods are symbolically arranged for the deceased and then a feast is held by the mourners in which both mourners and the dead eat together as the deceased embarks on their journey to the spirit world. At the end of the funeral, attendees are all given a piece of brown sugar candy, which is meant to erase the bad luck associated with attending a funeral, so that bad spirits or luck won't follow the person home.

Spirit Money and Spirit Houses

Because the afterlife in China replicates this life, it is believed that the dead will need all the things we need in this life—money, clothes, a car, a smartphone, food, and a house. Even status symbols are needed in the afterlife—men will often receive paper Rolex watches, while women will have the latest designer purse. When someone dies, their family will often visit a "paper store" where they can purchase paper and cardboard replicas of all the things they will need, including a large cardboard "doll house." Anything that the dead might have liked and/or needed in life will be bought for the dead in their afterlife, and it is the responsibility of the living to make sure that the dead are cared for and have all their necessary provisions. This is one reason why having children is so essential in Chinese culture—since they will be the ones to make regular offerings to keep you clothed and fed in your afterlife. Without children, the dead may soon find themselves wandering the underworld without clothes, a home, or food, and can become a hungry ghost.

CHRISTIAN MOURNING TRADITIONS

For Catholics, following the final interment of the body, the family usually retreats to the house of the family of the deceased, or to the parish hall of a Catholic church, where food is brought and a meal is shared while remembrance of the deceased occurs. Food, flowers, and gifts of money to help cover the funeral expenses are the most common gifts given to the family at and following the funeral. Extended family and friends usually gather as mourning functions as a negotiation and restructuring of social relations without the physical presence of the deceased. Scholar Tony Walter (2009) calls this model a framework of mourning based on "caring for the dead," rather than "remembering the dead." For this reason, most Catholic traditions of mourning and remembrance involve the (passive or active) participation of the deceased themselves in addition to the involvement of the extended social family structure. Catholics today don't wear special clothes to indicate they are in mourning, but some may still have a private altar in their homes to both worship God and honor the dead. This may be as simple as a picture of the deceased placed next to a crucifix or a rosary, and as elaborate as a small altar in the living room with multiple pictures, and material goods that the dead person cherished. The role of the Catholic after death is to recite **intercessory prayers** on behalf of the dead in order to ensure their safe passage from purgatory into heaven. This also ensures that the living are relying on God in this time of mourning, while giving the bereaved something to do on behalf of the dead besides grieving alone.

In the Catholic liturgical calendar, Ash Wednesday marks the beginning of the Lenten season and is meant to be a reflection on death, and the fact that all humans die. Most churches observe Lent, the forty-day reflection period observing Jesus' ministry and remembering his life and sacrifice, beginning with Ash Wednesday. In some churches, the leftover palm fronds from the previous year's Palm Sunday (the week before Easter, and a day meant to commemorate Jesus' entrance into Jerusalem) are taken and burned into ashes, which are then mixed with oil and placed in the sign of a cross on believer's foreheads in a ritual. A reminder of human mortality and the need for all Christians to reconcile with God in preparation for their death, the priest or pastor says (something along the lines of), "Remember you are dust, and to dust you shall return." The Ash Wednesday ritual is in many ways a reflection of the good death, and the call to live well, and to be ready to meet God, and be prepared for the final judgement. The Lenten season of forty days that follows Ash Wednesday and leads to the celebration of Easter, and the resurrection of Jesus, is meant to serve as an annual reflection on dying—and living—well.

In both the Catholic and Eastern Orthodox churches, it is common for the community to come together to share a meal following a funeral. This is an informal event in which the family and friends can come together to share their stories about the deceased and mourn together, and in the Orthodox tradition is called the **makaria**, which loosely translated means the "meal of blessings." The center dish served at the makaria is fish, since this was supposedly the first dish that Jesus ate following his resurrection. The fish is meant to symbolize and reenact the hope found in the resurrection, and to remind Orthodox believers that death does not triumph over life. Because one does not eulogize the dead at the funeral in the Orthodox tradition (only priests may offer prayers for and over the deceased, demonstrating their reliance upon God), it is at the makaria that friends and family share their stories and eulogize the deceased. In the Eastern Orthodox tradition, mourning lasts for forty days, and on the third, ninth, and fortieth day, it is customary to hold special memorial masses for the dead. Some Orthodox Christians believe that the soul will linger nearby for forty days, and sometimes visit their friends and family during that time in visions or dreams; after the final prayers on the fortieth day, they will undergo their final judgement. After the initial forty days, memorials are celebrated again at three months, six months, nine months, one year, and then every year on the anniversary of the death for a minimum of seven years. Generally, it is expected that close relatives of the deceased will mourn for one year, while spouses will also usually wear black mourning clothes and abstain from social gatherings during that time.

Protestant mourning customs are very diverse and dependent on various aspects such as class, geography, denomination, and environment, but most often there is a large repast following the funeral. There is generally little time off from work, with the bereavement period usually dictated by one's company or place of work, and people are frequently expected to return back to work and to their routines fairly quickly. The meal following the funeral, then, is often the only opportunity for gathering and remembering the deceased and re-situating the dead firmly in the past. It is also a time for the community to come together to remember the dead, while paying respects to the family and friends of the deceased. Generally, there are no standard Protestant mourning rituals, and the funeral itself will often be framed as a "**celebration of life**," rather than a funeral. In Protestantism, the deceased is believed to have been resurrected after their death to be with God, and thus the funeral is often viewed as an occasion for celebration and gratitude, rather than sorrow. For non-Protestants, this can be an unusual feature of the Protestant service, as it may seem as if the deceased person is particularly absent, and indeed, they are. For this reason, sometimes excessive grieving is not condoned, though there is great variation in this practice, with many African American churches adopting the practice of wailing or weeping as a way to demonstrate respect and care for the dead. Because of Protestant theological views, many funeral sermons will also be utilized as an opportunity to "spread the gospel," and may be used not only to tell the story of the deceased, but also to spread the Christian message and convert others into the faith.

NATIVE AMERICAN/INDIGENOUS MOURNING TRADITIONS

Native American mourning traditions are very diverse and vary greatly from tribe to tribe and place to place. Three examples of Indigenous practices will be examined here in order to give the reader a brief sample of the rich diversity found in native traditions—the Native Hawai'ian, North American Cherokee, and Alaskan Inuit—and will also be examined in Chapter 6 as well under afterlife conceptions and remembrance rituals. Following a death, native Hawai'ians usually dispose of the body with a partial cremation, after which the larger bones of a person are wrapped in ceremonial cloth by a priest, placed in a ceremonial basket and buried directly in the land in a traditional burial ground, or a cave. Called clean burial, a law was passed in 2015 to permit native Hawai'ians to use this form of disposal once again. Sometimes, in contemporary disposal practices, the cremains of a person are deposited in the ocean in a ceremony, oftentimes a paddle-out service where people ride canoes, surfboards, or other small ocean craft to accompany the cremains to their final resting place. Many people will sing songs (usually the song "Aloha 'Oe" is sung, which is a farewell song), offer prayers, and perform hulas, while wearing Aloha dress, or clothes in colorful Hawai'ian print. Traditionally, a funeral lament, known as **uwe helu**, was sung as someone was buried, and the lament was meant to both welcome the dead and to honor their life. Now, however, this custom seems to have almost disappeared and has been replaced by both singing and hula dancing. Funeral feasting also plays a role in mourning in Hawai'i, as traditional Hawai'ian foods are served to those participating in the mourning customs and funeral. Following a funeral, it is customary to sprinkle all those who attended (and the home of the deceased) with salt water in order to purify themselves and protect them from the dead, so that the dead don't follow them home and make trouble.

In the Cherokee tradition, a person prepares their clothes for burial in early adulthood. Known as their **dead clothes** (the clothes to be worn for burial), they are only brought out again when one is buried. Buried quickly after their death, most people were traditionally buried in fetal positions, either in earthen mounds, or in caves, but nowadays it is just as common to be buried on one's property, rather than in a public cemetery. Cherokee do not usually embalm their dead or donate their organs, and usually are buried directly in the earth. The body will be cleansed, anointed with lavender oil, which is believed to have healing properties, and then is buried with an eagle feather. Items of special significance are buried with the deceased individual, and are usually items the deceased might need in their afterlife journey such as food, water, and moccasins. Today, many funerals resemble more traditional American or Christian funerals, though there might be some prayers, songs, or traditional Cherokee dances as a part of the service. The mourning period after the burial usually lasts seven days, during which time members of the family should not express extreme emotions of joy or anger, and are expected to eat and drink little. As in native Hawai'ian culture, the house must be purified by a shaman, who purifies the house with tea and removes items that are seen as polluting from the home of the deceased. After the seven-day mourning period, the family of the deceased purifies themselves in river water seven times, after which they are given fresh clothing, and small gifts of tobacco and beads, and welcomed back into the tribal community. The one-week mourning period and the purification ceremony after are rituals that both allow the mourning family to grieve, and then to re-integrate themselves into the community after the death.

Similar to both native Hawai'ian and Cherokee traditions in the emphasis placed on purification, when someone dies in Inuit culture, the deceased is wrapped in a sealskin shroud, and then placed outside, while the family of the deceased empty the house of the belongings and then purify the home through cleaning and ritual fumigation. The body is then buried with their treasured belongings they might need in their afterlife. Men are buried with their head facing north, and women facing south, and a white rock is placed on top of the grave where the head is located. Like the Cherokee, those that handled the dead are expected to change clothes, or even throw away their clothes they wore while handling the body because they are considered to be polluted. Afterward, for the next five days, the mourners cry out to the dead, so they will return, and at the conclusion of the five-day mourning period, a firestone is thrown to the floor symbolizing the end of the grieving period, in a ritual called **iluraijuaqtut**. After the burial, people are not supposed to visit the graves for one year, and it is believed that the soul of the dead needs to be prepared before they can accept visitors (one example is that people must pass over the grave first without stopping—only once they have passed over it may they return to visit; this will ensure that sickness or bad luck does not follow the visitor back home). In all of these Indigenous mourning practices, one can see the importance of both purification and beliefs surrounding the dead as polluting or dangerous if practices are not observed with the proper rituals and care for the dead.

Religious mourning customs following a death vary widely, but across almost all religious traditions there are a few commonalities. Following a death, there are purification rituals intended to delineate the living from the dead, there are food traditions and hospitality exchanges meant to renegotiate relationships in the absence of the deceased, and there is a religious attempt at navigating meaning and feeling in the face of loss. In Chapter 6, we will turn to an examination of various afterlife conceptions and the ways those conceptions might impact remembrance rituals once the initial mourning period following a death has passed.

REFERENCES

Walter, Tony. "Communicating with the Dead," In C. Bryant & D. Peck, eds, *Death and the Human Experience*, Newbury Park, CA: Sage, 2009.

FOR FURTHER READING

Green, Laura C., and Martha Warren Beckwith. "Hawaiian customs and beliefs relating to sickness and death." *American Anthropologist* 28, no. 1 (1926): 176–208.

This is a wonderful article on native Hawai'ian death customs and beliefs.

Lili'uokalani Trust, "Hawaiian Grief Work," https://onipaa.org/kaumaha-helu-ekahi, last accessed May 2, 2022.

This is an informative, thought brief, website on Hawai'ian grief customs.

Sarhill, Nabeel, Susan LeGrand, Ramez Islambouli, Mellar P. Davis, and Declan Walsh. "The terminally ill Muslim: Death and dying from the Muslim perspective." *American Journal of Hospice and Palliative Medicine®* 18, no. 4 (2001): 251–255.

This article is a good summary of the Muslim views of death and dying from a Muslim perspective.

Thrane, Susan. "Hindu end of life: Death, dying, suffering, and karma." *Journal of Hospice and Palliative Nursing* 12, no. 6 (2010): 337–342.

This is a very succinct and helpful article on the intersection of Hindu beliefs and mourning.

AFTERLIVES AND AFTERDEATHS
Remembrance and Ritual

INTRODUCTION

In Chapter 5, we examined various religious mourning customs after death. In this chapter, we will turn to explore various conceptions and understandings of the afterlife in different religious traditions, and how these conceptions have, in turn, shaped thoughts on death and dying, and the ways in which people interpret death after life from a religious perspective. Focus here is placed on examining religious notions of afterlife and how those understandings intersect with death practices and the ways in which those practices then inform regular religious remembrance rituals practiced at large in the community. Since we addressed immediate mourning in Chapter 5, this one centers more on remembrance rituals and religious festivals centered on religious understandings of the afterlife. These regular liturgical memorialization practices serve to ground and reinforce religious worldviews.

JEWISH BELIEFS REGARDING THE AFTERLIFE

Generally, Jews do not concern themselves with beliefs or thoughts regarding an afterlife, although there are certain sects and individuals in Judaism who carry more defined beliefs about what occurs in the afterlife. Accordingly, there is generally a wide range of individual understandings of the afterlife found in Judaism, ranging from a belief in the final judgment and a resurrection of the dead, to a belief in reincarnation, to a belief of extinction. That being said, there are several traditional

DOI: 10.4324/9780429025075-6

remembrance rituals for the Jewish community regarding the dead. The purpose of Jewish rituals are for both the bereaved and the community, and they function as a way to reintegrate the Jewish dead into the community in their new roles as deceased, offering a way to honor the deceased so that their memory is recognized by the bereaved.

JEWISH REMEMBRANCE RITUALS

Kaddish is a Jewish prayer that celebrates the sanctification and power of God. The recitation of Kaddish originated in the eight century, as mention of this practice is mentioned in the Talmud text of Soferim. The Kaddish is widely recited during mourning as a way of emphasizing and demonstrating that even in mourning, one still worships God. One finds this theme throughout Judaism, particularly in regard to burial and observing shiva with regard to the sabbath and the observance of high holy days. Both the Sabbath and Jewish holidays take precedence over burial and mourning, as it is imperative that Jews worship God first and take care of worldly matters second. Kaddish is a continuance of this theme, in that its recitation reminds people that even in the midst of sorrow and mourning, God is great and worthy of praise. Additionally, some believe that offering Kaddish prayers will benefit the deceased, as merit accumulates on behalf of the deceased and thus the soul will not suffer (though this benefit is not directly mentioned, this is one of the common beliefs of the benefits of reciting Kaddish—that it will benefit not only the Jewish community of the bereaved, but also the soul of the deceased as well). In this way, it is not unlike the Roman Catholic purpose of reciting the rosary, which directly praises God, but is often indirectly believed to benefit the soul of the deceased so they will not suffer in purgatory). Traditionally, the Kaddish is said for the first year following a death, and then annually after that on the anniversary of the death. For other relatives and friends not part of the immediate family, the typical timeframe to recite the Kaddish is thirty days or one month. Since Jews traditionally pray three times a day (in the morning, afternoon, and evening), the Kaddish will usually be recited several times in the morning, both before and after the prayers, and then again in the afternoon and evening, following the prayers. Traditional Jewish law dictates that the son pray the Kaddish for his parents following their death, but if no son is available to recite the prayers, then sometimes the son-in-law or someone else is chosen to recite the prayers on the parents' behalf. This is changing to include women, and more women are reciting Kaddish for their families.

Yahrzeit is the celebration of the anniversary of a death, and on this day a twenty-four hour candle is lit at sundown, Kaddish prayers are recited, the dead are remembered, and the person remembering the dead foregoes any social events, sometimes fasting in remembrance. Most synagogues will also remember and honor the dead, with many modern synagogues lighting a lightbulb next to the person's name once a year in honor of the deceased and sending a notice to the family remembering their loved ones and reminding them of the yahrzeit. Often on the day of commemoration of the deceased, one visits the graveyard, recites the psalms, and is expected to lead the synagogue services as well. In this way, the dead are reincorporated into the realm of the living and provide a reason to reinforce the greater Jewish community. The remembrance of the dead thus occurs in three locations—the home, the synagogue, and the cemetery. If the death falls on a sabbath one year, then the candle is lit before sundown, and the grave is visited the day before or after the sabbath, so as not to interfere with worship. If the person chooses to fast in honor of yahrzeit but the death anniversary falls on a sabbath, then they must schedule their fasting on either the day prior to or the day after the Sabbath. If one forgets to observe the memorial, then one must observe yahrzeit as soon as it is remembered, and if one is too sick to observe the memorial, then someone else can observe it by proxy, lighting the candle and reciting the prayers in their place.

Yizkor is a special memorial prayer that is prayed four times a year for the deceased. It is recited after the Torah reading on the last day of Passover, the second day of Shavuot (the Jewish high holy day celebrating the giving of the Torah to the Jewish people), Shemini Atzeret (the eighth day of Sukkot), and on the Jewish day of atonement, Yom Kippur. The Hebrew word yizkor means to "remember," and Jews pray the yizkor to ask God to remember those family and friends who are deceased. Generally, those whose parents are both still living will leave the synagogue during the Yizkor service, and those who are in their first year of mourning (and therefore actively mourning, and not quite yet in the remembering or memorializing stage of their grief) will remain for the service but will not actually recite the Yizkor. In this way, the Jewish calendar accounts for the various stages of grief of the deceased, gradually moving the deceased from being actively mourned into more passive remembrances, while also helping the mourners through their grief by accompanying them ritually as a community. The prayer varies according to those for whom it is being prayed, but it is customary to not only pray the prayer in the synagogue, but also to attach a private vow to perform a charitable service in honor of the deceased, since the dead can no longer perform *mitzvot*, or kindnesses for others. This emphasis on charity mirrors the stress put on performing charitable works or giving donations on behalf of the deceased when someone initially dies. The importance of charity on behalf of someone who has died has two functions: (1) To perform deeds for the dead that they can no longer perform themselves, particularly a deed that they would have cared deeply about themselves, and (2) to remind the living that they remain in the world of the living and there is still work to do to make the world a better place—in short, to help the living re-map their place in the world without the dead by finding meaningful work that the dead would have valued and cared about.

Jewish Memorial Prayer

The prayer that follows is for a person's deceased father. (Chabad. org). "May G-d remember the soul of my father, my teacher (mention his Hebrew name and that of his mother) who has gone to his [supernal] world, because I will—without obligating myself with a vow—donate charity for his sake. In this merit, may his soul be bound up in the bond of life with the souls of Abraham, Isaac and Jacob, Sarah, Rebecca, Rachel and Leah, and with the other righteous men and women who are in Gan Eden; and let us say, Amen." Translation from Hebrew taken from Zalman Goldstein, "Yizkor—The Memorial Prayer," http://www.chabad.org/library/article_cdo/aid/371509/jewish/Yizkor-The-Memorial-Prayer.htm (accessed May 01, 2022).

MUSLIM BELIEFS REGARDING THE AFTERLIFE

In Islam, every life is sacred and considered to be a gift from God. Also, just as one lives, everyone will one day die. As the Qur'an states, "Every soul shall have a taste of death: In the end to us shall you be brought back (29:57)." Like Christians, Muslims believe in a day of judgement when one dies, but unlike Christianity, **deathbed confessions**, confessions of transgressions against God and others as one is dying, are not necessarily viewed as sincere (Constantine, for example, is famous for having confessed his most heinous sins on his deathbed right before his deathbed baptism). As in Judaism, one must first ask forgiveness of one's sins from the people one has harmed, and forgiveness from God for those sins against God, throughout one's life, and not wait until the last moment before death. The confession of sins is meant to function as a way to cleanse one's soul, but is viewed as more productive if practiced regularly throughout one's life. That being said, the dying are encouraged to recite the **Shahadah** before one's death. One of the five pillars of Islam, the recitation of the Shahadah states that "There is no God but Allah and Muhammad is his messenger," and is an active confirmation of the belief in Allah, and in Muhammad who is considered to be the last and final prophet. Like confession, the daily and regular recitation of the shahadah affirms one's commitment to Islam and is not limited to one's dying days.

It is believed that once the deceased are buried, they will then be given, or returned, to God. As the Qur'an states, "Indeed we belong to Allah, and Indeed to him we will return" (2:156). For most Muslims, the return to God is one that holds a promise of a judgement, **Yawm al-din**, over all right and wrong that one has committed in their lifetime. Like Christianity, a belief in a final judgement and resurrection are both key to the Muslim understanding of life after death. **Akhirah** is the Muslim term to describe one's life after death in Islam. Heaven, or **Jannah** (literally, paradise), is described multiple times in the Qur'an as a garden, where one can be reunited with other loved ones, and does not feel pain, sickness, or sadness. Descriptions of hell, or **Jahannam,** depict a place of physical and spiritual suffering, and a place where souls go to undergo punishment for their sins. It is believed that the dead are questioned by angels after their death during their final judgement so it is often customary for people to stay a while in the cemetery near the grave to pray prayers of supplication on behalf of the deceased.

Less stressed in contemporary Islamic thought, traditional belief dictates that the dead inhabit an in-between world called **Barzakh**, where one has a temporary body and awaits judgment. There are many different descriptions of Barzakh, and some describe it as a type of Muslim purgatory, since some believe it is a place where souls can be prayed for and have earthly deeds ascribed to them while waiting for God's judgment (Afikul Islam, 2008). For the most part, contemporary Muslim theologians tend to de-emphasize Barzakh and instead stress the need for individual accountability at the moment of judgement. That being said, it remains important to follow the rituals regarding the disposal of the dead, for it is believed that every act on behalf of the dead can affect their judgment in the afterlife.

MUSLIM REMEMBRANCE RITUALS

In Islam, there are several key dates following a death: Three days, seven days, forty days, and finally a year. These are all important dates and outline a mourning trajectory that often moves from intense grief to **integrated grief** (the technical term used to describe someone who has learned how to live and function with their grief). Three days of mourning is the standard practice observed by almost all Muslims, and this period is an intense mourning period in which family and friends will come and care for the family of the deceased. On both the seventh and fortieth days following the burial, and again one year later, it is customary for family and friends to come together to hold a memorial to offer prayers, recite the Qur'an, do charitable works in honor of the deceased, and offer donations in their memory. There are also some who believe that on the seventh and fortieth days following a death, the soul of the deceased will return to visit their loved ones in their home, though this seems to be more of a popular Muslim belief, and not one that is scripturally based in the Qur'an. Whatever one believes, the ritualized custom of the community coming together at regular intervals to support the bereaved and to offer charity and prayers on behalf of the deceased allows the living to believe that they can aid the dead in their afterlife, which may in turn be helpful for continuing bonds and healthy grief.

Muslim Condolence Prayer

وَلْتَحْتَسِبْ فَلْتَصْبِرْ . ً مُسَمَّى . بِأَجَلٍ " عِنْدَهُ شَيْءٍ وَكُلُّ أَعْطَى، مَا " وَلَهُ أَخَذَ، مَا للهِ إِنَّ
لِمَيْتِكَ وَغَفَرَ عَزَاءَكَ، وَأَحْسَنَ أَجْرَكَ، اللهُ أَعْظَمَ

154. 'Verily to Allah, belongs what He took and to Him belongs what He gave, and everything with Him has an appointed time… and then he ordered for her to be patient and hope for Allah's reward.'

One can also say:

May Allah magnify your reward, make better your solace and forgive your deceased.

Note: This is the saying of some of the scholars, not a hadeeth.

(Islamic Burial Prayers)

HINDU BELIEFS REGARDING THE AFTERLIFE

Hindu beliefs regarding the afterlife center around the idea of **samsara**, and the idea that one's soul, or **atman**, is reborn in a different body following one's death. The belief in reincarnation is often likened to changing clothes. One's essential self stays the same, but the body one "wears" changes with each lifetime. Hindus believe that one's **karma** determines one's rebirth, and that each life will have a different lesson. The notion of karma here is important as it is used to both justify and explain suffering. When one suffers a disability or misfortune, people will point to one's karma, and the lessons that must be learned in this lifetime in retribution for a misdeed in one's last lifetime (the same can be said for positive karma; one's wealth or fortune can be due to positive karma accrued in one's last lifetime). As a result, one's karma is directly responsible for one's rebirth. Some Hindus believe that rebirth happens almost immediately following a death, while others believe that an atman may exist in other realms for a while before being reborn. Thus, like the Buddhist notion of the afterlife, the Hindu understanding of heaven and hell is also a temporal realm where one's soul may reside for a period of time either reaping the benefits or suffering the consequences of one's karma.

HINDU REMEMBRANCE RITUALS

The shraddha ceremony is conducted on the tenth day following a death, monthly, and then annually on the anniversary of the death, when it is believed that the dead person will join the greater pantheon of dead ancestors, or **pitri**. The shraddha ceremony is an important ritual as it marks the transition of the soul from wandering spirit to ancestor, and ensures that the dead person has made the transition from liminality to ancestor. Children are expected to annually honor their mothers and fathers separately on the anniversary of their deaths, and the shraddha is meant to serve as a ritual of not only remembrance, but also gratitude. In honor of the deceased, the family of the deceased will give to charity, since it is believed that all charity and food given in the name of the deceased will eventually reach the dead themselves. In this way, the living are able to care for the dead and ensure their safe passage to a new rebirth. The shraddha ceremony is usually led by a Brahmin priest, and with the male heir of the deceased. In the ceremony, one offers food to the ancestors, consisting of rice balls made of rice, milk, ghee (clarified butter), black sesame seeds, and honey, which are then mixed into small rice balls and fed to crows, who symbolize the ancestors returning in animal form to eat. In this ceremony, the living continue to care for the dead, who are hungry and need nourishment as their souls move through their afterlife journey. Finally, a brief fire ceremony is performed, which helps to ensure that the offerings will be transmitted to the dead souls.

In addition to the personal remembrance ceremonies, Hindus celebrate **pitru paksha**, an annual sixteen-day period in honor of all of one's ancestors. Determined by the lunar calendar, it usually falls somewhere in the month of September, on or near the autumnal equinox. During this ceremony, the names of the previous three generations, the present generation, and the two generations below one's generation (six altogether) are recited, affirming one's place in this world, and one's past and future. Food offerings are made, consisting of kheer (sweet rice and milk), lentils, and pumpkin, along with the rice balls that are fed to the crows. The annual celebration of pitru paksha thus serves to affirm the ties between the living and the dead through food exchanges.

The Story of Karna and Feeding the Dead

The Hindu story of Karna explains the need to feed the dead. Karna, who died in the war of the Mahabarata, was known to be extremely generous in his lifetime, but while he gave gold and clothes and other riches, he never donated food. When Karna died, because he never donated food, he had much wealth and many riches in his afterlife, but could never find food, and was always hungry. For this reason, when he was reborn, he vowed to donate food so that all who died would not be hungry. To this day, Hindus make sure to offer food to the dead so they will not be hungry as they wait to be reborn.

SIKH BELIEFS REGARDING THE AFTERLIFE

Sikhs believe that when one dies, the individuality of self is lost. Heaven and hell do not exist as concepts, though like Hindus and Buddhists, Sikhs do believe in reincarnation and the notion that one may be reborn to learn lessons or improve their karma. But like Islam, Sikhism also believes in an eternal, all-loving God and the ultimate goal of a Sikh is to learn one's lessons in life so that they might be united with God for eternity after death. Reincarnation is only a temporary state for those who have not yet learned everything they need to learn before reuniting with God. For this reason, many Sikhs believe that being reincarnated into a human life is an opportunity to learn about right from wrong and good from evil, and one must take advantage of one's life to learn as much as possible and to perform good deeds so that they might be reunited with Waheguru upon one's death. For this reason, death is viewed as a release and possible reunification with God, and thus should not be overtly mourned, as this might be viewed as a questioning of God's will.

SIKH REMEMBRANCE RITUALS

Sikh mourning rituals generally do not center on the deceased, but rather focus on God. Mourners are encouraged to chant God's name (Waheguru) as a sign of calling on God, and to rely on him in addition to reading Sikh scriptures, which are intended to remind the family of their reliance of God and trust in his will. On the first anniversary of a death, the family will gather to pray, eat, and celebrate the life of the deceased, reciting the **Barsi** prayer, and then sharing a meal together. Punjabi for "death anniversary," the Barsi prayer is a one-year commemoration for the deceased on the anniversary of their death. Usually friends and family gather and recite Sikh scriptures, share a meal together, and offer stories about their loved one who has died. Reciting the Barsi prayer is meant to serve not only those in mourning, but is also viewed as an opportunity to pray for the deceased and to offer intercessory support to the dead. It also offers a predictable timeframe for those in mourning, while aiding them with community support.

BUDDHIST BELIEFS REGARDING THE AFTERLIFE

The Buddhist view of the afterlife varies dependent on the school of Buddhism, as well as its cultural context (the bardos in Tibetan Buddhism, for example, differ greatly from the Pureland found in Chinese Buddhism), but in general, Buddhists believe in **samsara**, the endless cycle of life, death, and rebirth. In this worldview, one's soul is reborn over and over in a series of repetitive lifecycles as one seeks to learn the lessons one is supposed to learn. Ultimately, the goal of a Buddhist is to reach **nirvana**, or enlightenment, leading to the cessation of the soul's participation in the endless cycle of life, death, and rebirth. Since the goal is release from this endless cycle through the cessation of self, the notion of afterlife in Buddhism—and the heavens and hells that make up the rich afterlife imaginaries—functions differently than in Christianity or Islam. In Buddhism, heaven and hell are considered to be temporal, liminal places where one's soul spends time on its journey to the next life as they finish learning the lessons (through rewards or punishment) from one's last lifetime. One's **karma**, or actions from one's lifetime(s), determine one's rebirth, and heaven can be a place where one can be reborn because of positive karma, while hell is a place to be punished for one's past misdeeds. Only humans, though, can escape the cycle of samsara altogether, which is why it is ultimately better to be reborn a human than to become a divine being in heaven. This can be particularly difficult for Christians or Muslims to understand, as they have not been raised with an understanding of an afterlife that is only viewed as a stepping stone to a more elusive goal. Thus, in Buddhism, the afterlife is not the ultimate goal; but rather, the ultimate goal is the cessation of self and escape from rebirth.

BUDDHIST REMEMBRANCE RITUALS

Buddhist remembrance rituals generally center on the first forty-nine days, as it is believed that a soul is reborn on the forty-ninth day, or seven weeks following a death. Thus, the remembrance rituals during this initial seven weeks are meant to function as a sort of religious intervention in which the family and friends of the deceased and the Buddhist community in general, regularly come together to pray, make offerings, and say prayers to ensure the best possible rebirth. The **sangha**, or the Buddhist clergy, and the lay community demonstrate a mutually interdependent relationship, as the family and community often make food and money donations to the sangha in return for the clergy's prayers on behalf of, and for, the deceased. On the one hundredth day, there is often another ceremony in celebration of the deceased's passing into their new life, often marked by foods that the deceased enjoyed in their lifetime. Finally, the death is again honored at the one-year anniversary, with incense, prayers, food offerings, and special chants by the community in honor of the deceased. Like the Catholic memorial mass, this one-year anniversary serves to ritually honor and care for the dead, ensuring the reciprocal relationship between both the living and the dead, while reinforcing the ties between the lay community and the Buddhist clergy.

Though they vary widely, most Buddhist cultures also have annual remembrance ceremonies for the dead in which the living regularly honor and pray for the dead, and include the wider pantheon of unremembered or unrecognized dead. These annual festivities recognize all the dead that might have been forgotten by the living, or for whom there is no one remaining to make offerings on their behalf. They also include more marginalized deaths, such as those who die by accident, or those who died from unfortunate circumstances, such as by homicide or suicide. Annual

Buddhist festivals for the dead allow the larger community to care for all the dead—both remembered and forgotten—and serve the community through protecting and purifying the realm by honoring the dead. The reciprocal relationship between the living and the dead becomes regularly and ritually reinforced through annual festivities honoring and caring for the dead. In China, this day is known as **Qing Ming**, or the tomb sweeping day, and on this day people return to their ancestral tomb and clean the tombs and make ritual offerings of food and prayer. In Japan, the annual **Bon Odori** is celebrated in honor of one's ancestors, and it is believed that the dead return to visit with their relatives and eat their favorite foods. Similarly, in Thailand, **Gin Salat** is a festival in which people give offerings and favorite household items needed in their afterlife to the deceased. In short, most Buddhist cultures celebrate some form of annual commemoration of and for the dead, with offerings from the religious (prayers) to the mundane (material objects needed in the afterlife).

CHINESE BELIEFS REGARDING THE AFTERLIFE

In China, traditional views of the soul assert that the soul has three essential parts—a part that is buried with the body in the grave (known as **po**), a part that is placed in the ancestral tablet (and called **hun**), and a third part that goes on to the Ten Courts of Judgement, or Ten Courts of Hell, and is eventually reborn. The part that goes on to the Chinese underworld undertakes a journey where one's rewards and punishments are meted out according to one's deeds in their lifetime. Unlike the Abrahamic faiths where the judgement is permanent, the underworld journey is more like the Buddhist view—a temporary place where one resides before being reborn. Regular sacrifices, prayers, and offerings need to be made at both the ancestral grave and at the ancestral tablet in order to ensure that the departed dead become spirits, or **shen**, who have the ability to care for and help the living, in a similar way that the living have the ability to care for the deceased. If the ancestors are not properly cared for by the living, they can become **gui**, or ghosts, who can, and often will, haunt the living. Thus, in the Chinese worldview, the worlds of the living and the dead are interdependent and mutually dependent. The dead will help the living as long as the living care for the dead. Thus, remembrance rituals in China are absolutely essential.

CHINESE REMEMBRANCE RITUALS

Following a death, regular sacrificial rites are undertaken in honor of the dead; these are conducted daily at first, and then at bi-monthly and annual services. The tablets of the deceased are kept in the ancestral hall of a home, and are generally housed in a hierarchical order similar to the realm of the living, from oldest to youngest, and male to female. Regular food offerings, incense, and prayers are offered to the tablets, with particular attention paid to annual anniversaries of the death. Special offerings are sometimes made on festivals or occasions of joy (such as weddings and/or births) in gratitude to the ancestors for their special protection or blessings. These acts of veneration are made because of the Chinese concept of **filial piety**, or **xiao**, which is the concept that there is reciprocity between family members based on age, hierarchy, and mutual respect (e.g., father to son, mother to daughter, elder brother to younger sister, etc.). Likewise, the dead are expected to care for the living, and in return the living should remember and honor the dead. The relationship between the living and dead is a reciprocal and interdependent one.

Apart from regular rituals on specific death anniversaries, **qing ming** is the primary festival of the dead. Qing Ming, or tomb-sweeping day, as it is sometimes known, is celebrated on the fifteenth day after the spring equinox. On this day, families return to their ancestral tombs, clean the burial sites, and make offerings of prayers, incense, spirit money, paper goods, wine, and food. A public holiday in mainland China, the holiday is celebrated across the Chinese diaspora, and in Malaysia, Thailand, Vietnam, Taiwan, and Singapore. Although qing ming is celebrated in Buddhist cultures as well as Confucian ones, it is considered to be primarily a Confucian and secular tradition in contemporary mainland China. Because many people travel long distances on qing ming, the holiday is also known for the serving of cold foods, particularly glutinous rice dumplings, known as **qingtuan**. Some folk stories say that serving glutinous rice will make the ancestors happy and their mouths will stick together so that they can only give good reports about the living to the gods of the spirit world; more likely, it was simply a food that could transport easily, while also having a longer shelf life.

CHRISTIAN BELIEFS REGARDING THE AFTERLIFE

Like Muslims, Catholics, Orthodox Christians, and Protestants believe in a **final judgment**—the belief that when one dies, one's soul leaves one's body to stand before God for a weighing of one's good and bad deeds from one's lifetime. The soul is then sent to either reside in heaven or in hell; Catholics have the added in-between state of **purgatory**, and this singular belief informs nearly all the practices surrounding the care for and remembrance of the dead among Catholics. Purgatory is a place where one's soul is sent if one's positive deeds do not necessarily outweigh the negative ones (or in theological terms, if one's sins are too great to go straight to heaven). It can be difficult for non-Catholic Christians to understand purgatory and the practices surrounding its belief, but it is from the belief in purgatory, that the practices of saying rosaries, celebrating masses for the dead, offering anniversary masses for the deceased, and observing the holidays of All Souls' Day emerge. All of these practices are meant to help the deceased move from purgatory into heaven, while also allowing the functional purpose of giving the bereaved something to actively *do* in honor of the dead. In the Protestant worldview, the dead are not located in a place where they need help or the living are able to offer assistance to the dead. One of the big shifts in this belief in the afterlife, particularly in the last hundred years, has been a decrease in the belief of hell as a possible outcome for the afterlife of the dead (Walter, 2009). This has led to decreased participation in practices regarding the dead; if the bereaved believe their loved one has moved straight to heaven, then there is little need to spend the time and/or money committing to rituals surrounding the dead.

CATHOLIC REMEMBRANCE RITUALS

Catholicism encourages regular **masses for the dead**, services in which prayers for the dead are offered, particularly on significant dates following the death. While one might be morally certain of the deceased's place in heaven, masses help provide additional assurance through the prayers of the living. Toward this end, it is common to not only recite rosaries for the deceased, but to petition for masses to be dedicated to the deceased. Thus, if the deceased is Catholic, usually one's family will honor the dead with masses on the third, seventh, and thirtieth days following a death or a funeral (the count of days begin with the day immediately following the date of death or the day of burial; both days are appropriate starting points), and then annually after that. Small stipends (usually somewhere around $5 or $10) are given to the priest to recite the mass, and generally, a card is given to the family who has requested the mass for the dead in acknowledgement. This card is somewhat like a greeting card and tells the receiver that her deceased loved one has had a mass recited in their honor. In between masses for the dead, it is common practice for the bereaved to light a candle (with a small token payment) at the church in honor of the deceased, and to offer prayer in memory of the dead.

It is also common practice to pass out **prayer cards** in honor of the dead at the funeral or the anniversary mass for the dead. Often these contain a picture of the deceased, with their birth and death dates on one side, and a prayer of intercession for their soul on the other side. These cards are usually handed out so that attendees of both the funeral and mass for the dead might pray for the deceased. With the Internet, it is now becoming easier for families to sign up for intercessory masses online, or to have candles lit for them in prayer at churches (also for a small donation). In this way, many traditional Catholic practices are moving online. Finally, it is common for Catholics to place small notices in the local paper for important anniversaries of the death (usually at one year, five years, ten years, fifteen years, etc.), in which the family honors the deceased with a short message to and about the deceased, and if they are Catholic, announcing the time and place of the anniversary mass. Often the messages are short but illuminating, and like obituaries, tend to privilege immediate family members and their relationship to the deceased. As the Internet replaces the newspaper as the primary medium for news, many families now use more informal channels, like social media, to remind others of the remembrances of the dead and announcements of masses.

Catholic Intercessory Prayer for the Dead

In your hands, O Lord,
we humbly entrust our brothers and sisters.
In this life you embraced them with your tender love;
deliver them now from every evil
and bid them eternal rest.
The old order has passed away:
welcome them into paradise,
where there will be no sorrow, no weeping or pain,
but fullness of peace and joy
with your Son and the Holy Spirit
forever and ever.
R/. Amen. (United States Conference of Catholic Bishops. n.d.)

Apart from the annual anniversary of the death of the deceased, November 2, or **All Souls' Day**, is the most important regular annual service for the dead, with Catholic families gathering in homes, at the graves, and in churches to remember and pray for the dead. While **Día de los Muertos**, or Day of the Dead, is becoming widely known, it must be stressed that this holiday is primarily a Mexican and Mexican American holiday, with many Spanish speaking countries celebrating All Souls' Day, but not Día de los Muertos. Originating in Catholic beliefs in Purgatory, and the need to intercede on behalf of the dead, St. Cluny is credited with first establishing the practice of observing All Souls' Day on November 2, 998 CE. Observing the practice of praying for the dead soon spread to the rest of the Cluniac order before spreading to Southern Europe, and then in the fourteenth century to Rome. Originally only one day of intercession for the dead, it was not long before the November 2 observance spread to cover the entire month of November, with names of the deceased prayed over in masses for the dead and including October 31 (All Saints' Eve), November 1 (All Saints' Day), and November 2 (All Souls' Day). When the Spanish colonialists settled in Mexico in 1519, the Roman Catholic tradition was fused with Indigenous Aztec tradition remembering the dead through reverence of the goddess Mictecacihuatl, known more contemporaneously as the **Lady of the Dead**. The images of the Lady of the Dead are not that different from those of the Grim Reaper popular in Europe in the sixteenth century, and serve as a reminder that death is commonplace.

DÍA DE LOS MUERTOS

The Mexican Day of the Dead, or **Día de los Muertos**, emerged from the popular Catholic practice of memorializing the dead in the Catholic Feast celebrating All Souls' Day. It is believed that the sugar skulls characterizing the celebration of the remembrance for the dead in Mexico emerged from the socio-political landscape at the time. Abundant in sugar, but poor in capital, Mexicans wanted to adorn their churches with similar church decorations popular with their colonialist conquerors, turning to sugar's malleable properties to make colorful and edible decorations for the church and home altars. In addition to sugar skulls, marigold flowers often adorn the graves, altars, and churches to remember the dead. It is believed that the colors, earth tones, help to guide the dead home, and return the souls safely to their homes and altars. In addition, it is common to bake **Pan de Muerto** buns, or Day of the Dead bread, made with flour, butter, sugar, eggs, orange peel, anise, and yeast. The Pan de Muerto buns, sugar skulls, and oranges are offered at the family altars along with pictures of the deceased, candles, and flowers.

In Mexico, graveyards are publicly owned, and it is the community's responsibility to maintain the graveyard, with church members and families coming together to pull weeds, and tend to the graves, leaving offerings of food and flowers at the tomb. The Mexican graveyard, because of its proximity next to or near the church, is often situated at the center of public space, making its maintenance doubly important. Conversely, because most graveyards in the United States are privately owned, and some with set visiting hours, Mexican Americans living in the United States have tended to honor the deceased with a home altar, and the grave itself as the nexus of the social sphere has been relegated to the more private sphere of the nuclear family home. Thus, while Mexican American graves are still visited and maintained, they have not retained the same function as gravesites in Mexico, where the cemetery is both literally and figuratively the center of the world of the living and the dead. In Mexico, on Día de los Muertos, the family brings chairs, tables, food, drink, flowers, candles, and pictures, feasting in the cemetery with extended family both alive and dead, spending the day with the present family telling stories about the dead family, saying prayers for the souls of the dead, and giving offerings of both food and drink. The functional purpose is to remind those who are alive that life is short, and to connect the living with the stories of the dead, situating their place in this world through narrative and the fixed location of the tomb. Thus, even those Mexicans and Mexican Americans who are Protestant may still participate in the cultural aspects of the Día de los Muertos tradition, focusing on the parts of this holiday that emphasize Mexican heritage and culture.

EASTERN ORTHODOX BELIEFS REGARDING THE AFTERLIFE

Eastern Orthodox Christians believe that death separates the soul from the body, with the body returning to the earth, and at the moment of the final judgement, the soul and body will be reunited with each other (this is why cremation is forbidden in the Orthodox Church) for the final judgement by God. However, the Orthodox Church generally refrains from theological speculation regarding the afterlife, electing instead to focus on the certainty of salvation through Christ, the rejection of reincarnation, and affirming the importance of reciting prayers for the dead so that they are not forgotten. For this reason, like Catholicism, masses for the dead play an important and vital role in the Orthodox Church, along with iconography. **Icons** are depictions of Jesus, Mary, the saints, angels, and other holy personages. The Greek word for Icon, Αγιογραφία, can be broken into two words meaning "to write what is holy." In other words, icons are meant to be viewed as a window into heaven, and are meant to be visual tools that help believers envision a holy world that translates concepts such as "heaven" into possible realities. Iconography is one of the distinguishing characteristics of Eastern Orthodoxy, and they are painted in such a way to purposely make the spectator imagine and realize the ethereal. In this way, icons can serve as spiritual tools to help people better imagine an afterlife after death.

EASTERN ORTHODOX REMEMBRANCE RITUALS

Prayer services for the dead play a major role in the religious life of an Orthodox person, along with the memorial wheat dish, koliva, discussed in Chapter 3. Koliva plays a role not only in the initial funeral service, but is served at all Orthodox memorial services as well, and its ingredients are meant to remind Orthodox followers of the resurrection. Recipes vary based on location and family tradition, but the koliva almost always includes wheat, dried fruit, and some type of sweetener—usually honey or sugar. The wheat comes from Jesus' words regarding death and resurrection from John 12:24 "Very truly I tell you, unless a kernel of wheat falls to the ground and dies, it remains only a single seed. But if it dies, it produces many seeds" (NIV Study Bible). The wheat then reminds one that it is only through death that one can be resurrected and reunited with God. The fruit in the dish symbolizes the risen Christ, and serves as a reminder to followers that they too will experience the sweetness of being reunited with God. The koliva thus serves as a material, and sensory reminder, of the Christian scriptures and the promise of redemption and life after death.

PROTESTANT BELIEFS REGARDING THE AFTERLIFE

The dominant Protestant, largely evangelical, Christian view of the afterlife is that when one dies, they will be sent before God to have one's life reviewed, and then based on one's good and bad deeds throughout one's life, they will either be sent for the rest of eternity to **heaven** or **hell**. The depictions of these eternal places vary, from heaven as a place where one is simply in the presence of God, to elaborate kingdoms where one will be reunited with one's ancestors and loved ones who have died before. Similarly, there are also many variations of the understanding of hell—from a hell in which one is eternally separated from God to a fiery pit with active and eternal punishment by a fallen angel demon that resides over one's various condemnations. The time of judgment varies between denominations, with some denominations believing in a judgment that occurs immediately upon one's death, to others proclaiming that judgment will be delayed until the second coming of Christ, when it is believed that all the dead will once again be resurrected and then judged.

This idea of **resurrection** is important, because it the belief that one's body is central to the resurrection that informs the corresponding belief that one's body should be intact in order to be able to be resurrected. And it is because of this belief that both body and the soul are needed to be able to be resurrected that Protestants sometimes view cremation and organ donation with suspicion, though this is shifting. Theological justifications for cremation and organ donation now emphasize belief that the earthly body will be exchanged for a new heavenly body. While grossly generalizing and reducing the metaphysical argument behind the theology for the sake of simplifying the overall concepts here, it should be noted that this theological shift is also occurring at a time of great medical advances and a more general acceptance of organ transplantation and donation, in addition to genetic testing. It remains a "chicken and the egg" kind of problem, in that one can trace cultural shifts in attitudes toward death and the afterlife and trace corresponding theological interpretations to medical and cultural advances.

PROTESTANT REMEMBRANCE RITUALS

Among Protestants, **memorialization**—or personal ways in which the living honor the dead—can be extremely important, as it is through the rituals honoring the dead that the living can reaffirm the ties that bind the larger community. It should be noted too that these practices are usually highly individuated, and are more concerned with remembering, than caring for, the dead (unlike Catholicism which seeks to maintain some ties between the dead and the living). Generally, candles, teddy bears, balloons, or flowers are left in remembrance of the deceased, either at the place of burial/disposition, or at the site of the death. The variety found in Protestant memorialization practices reveals the importance of the individual and DIY memorial culture. Protestantism's emphasis on free will and individual interpretation also points to a lack of social and religious cohesion with no overarching social grammar to govern mourning rituals. In other words, Protestants may have more freedom and ability to individuate their bereavement customs according to what works for them, but the lack of a unified social norm can also leave some feeling unmoored during their mourning.

Interesting to note, African American Protestants generally visit the graves of the deceased on a much more regular basis than their white counterparts, bringing flowers and other material offerings (most often personal effects owned by the deceased while she was living; this may include such personal and trivial things such as a toothbrush, cup, or favorite toy) to leave at the grave marker for the deceased. The importance of not only marking the grave, but having a place to return where one can acknowledge the death of the deceased, is an important part of contemporary African American Protestant grief culture. Sometimes, family and friends bring a drink (usually alcohol), and pour the drink directly onto the grave of the deceased so that the deceased may once again celebrate with her loved ones in her afterlife. This tradition goes back to older traditions of offering libations at the gravesite of the deceased, and again, offers a chance for the grieving to somehow "care for the dead" while simultaneously interacting with them (Sullivan, 1995).

NATIVE AMERICAN/INDIGENOUS BELIEFS REGARDING THE AFTERLIFE

Indigenous beliefs regarding the afterlife vary from tribe to tribe and place to place. Native Hawai'ian beliefs will vary greatly from Cherokee, which will vary vastly from Alaskan Inuit beliefs. That being said, in many Indigenous traditions, it is commonly believed that souls pass from the world of the living into a spirit realm, where they occasionally visit the world of the living and communicate with them through dreams of spirit possession. A few examples illustrate the wide diversity in afterlife beliefs between Indigenous peoples. Native Hawai'ians believe that a person's soul, or **'uhane**, can wander away from one's body in life, visiting others in their dreams. Likewise, after death, the soul leaves the body and proceeds to the afterlife or the underworld ('Ao'ao mau o ka honua or the "everlasting side of the earth"). The afterlife is believed to be similar to this life. Those souls with exceptional spiritual power, or **mana**, might become **'amakua**, or guardian spirits for the family. The 'amakua are responsible for being spiritual guides to the living, and often escort those who die into the afterlife. Like many other cultures, there is also a belief in wandering spirits, or lapu, who can operate as potentially mean or dangerous tricksters to the living. In addition, many contemporary Hawai'ian folktales still circulate today about the night marchers, or **huaka'i pō**, dead warriors who used to serve the Hawai'ian chief. It is believed that if one comes across them, or does something **kapu**, or taboo, then the nightmarchers will punish them with a violent death. These stories really serve as a narrative way to safeguard traditional Hawai'ian beliefs and sacred places, by offering punishments to those that don't take them seriously.

The Cherokee believe that there are four souls in the body, and as a result, there are four corresponding stages of death. The first is the conscious soul, which leaves immediately following a death, and is located in the person's head (this might interestingly enough, correspond with contemporary definitions of brain death), and is a large part of why the practice of scalping one's enemies originally emerged, since scalping was viewed as an attack of one's soul. The second soul is located in the liver, and is viewed as the soul of physiological life. The third soul is located in the heart, and it is believed that this soul takes a month to die. The fourth soul resides in the bones, and it is believed that this soul lingers in bones for up to a year. This corresponds with the mourning calendar in the Cherokee tradition, during which one is expected to tend to the grave and keep it free of weeds for one year. After a year, it is believed that nothing of significance is left at the grave, and at that time, one is released from mourning.

Alaskan Inuits believe that after death, human souls go to either an upper world in the sky, which is warm with plenty of food, or to an underworld (in the sea), where people will suffer from the cold and not have enough to eat. Death was mostly viewed as a transition to a new existence, one that was mostly determined not by whether one was a good or bad person, but rather by how one died. A woman who died in childbirth, or a man who died at sea would be assured of an afterlife in the sea, rather than the sky. Greenland Inuits even believe that people can reappear in the realm of the living as ghosts. The many beliefs regarding the afterlife among Indigenous peoples are as rich as they are varied.

INDIGENOUS REMEMBRANCE RITUALS

After the initial funeral and mourning, remembrance rituals also vary across Indigenous traditions. In Hawai'i, it is customary to observe the one-year anniversary following a death. A funeral feast, the **'aha'aina waimaka** (literally translated as a feast of tears) is held exactly one year following a death and is meant to both recognize the end of one year of mourning, while also symbolizing a new beginning following the one-year mourning period. Traditional foods served at the feast center around the pig, or pua'a—a ritual offering for the gods. Thus, one will almost always find pork, fish (considered to be the "sea pig"), and taro (in Hawai'i, taro leaves are the vegetable symbol of the pig, and the first Hawai'ian was said to be born as a taro). Nowadays, there is usually a funeral feast, and traditional lu'au foods are served, which usually include these same dishes. During mourning, the family is encouraged to focus on healing through a focus on **ho'oponopono** or "setting it right." In traditional Hawai'ian culture, the practice of ho'oponopono means to tidy up, to restore balance, and to ensure healing so that one can feel whole again.

Similar to the native Hawai'ian practices, the Cherokee traditionally used the one-year anniversary of a death to mark the end of the core mourning period, and it is at that time that the soul has made its transition from the body. As in all native traditions, the most important aspect in remembrance is the concern with pollution from the dead, and a focus on taboos that might impact and disrupt the realm of the living. Today, the Cherokee honor their Cherokee nation on March 24, officially known as **Cherokee Nation Remembrance Day**, remembering the deaths of many who died under the forced relocation in the Trail of Tears, when the American government forcibly removed the Native Americans from their homes and relocated them a thousand miles away. Though not centered on individual deaths, this day honors the many deaths of the Cherokee nation, while serving as a commemoration of the Cherokee community and its many losses suffered as a people under American aggression.

The most common ceremony held in remembrance of the dead among Northwest tribes, including the Inuit, is the potlatch, a feast held both immediately following a death, and one year later on the anniversary of the death. The potlatch also functioned as a way to bring tribes together to redistribute wealth, bestow status, and rank on people, and to clarify claims to territory used for hunting and/or fishing. Essentially, they were large tribal meetings in which hospitality exchanges served to cement one's status and create alliances. The potlatch that was held immediately following a death often served to resituate family identity following a death, and depending on the status of the deceased, sometimes the community would take down and rebuild a home so that the family could reestablish their dwelling without pollution from the deceased. One year following a death, many communities hold a potlatch in honor of the deceased, beginning with the singing of memorial songs and various speeches, before serving favorite foods of the deceased. Also, food gifts and blankets are given to guests attending the potlatch, and sometimes, money is also given in thanks for help at the time of funeral. In 1884, Canada outlawed potlatches, followed by the United States in 1885, and it was not until 1951 in Canada and 1934 in the United States, that the restriction against potlatches was lifted and the Northwestern tribes were once again allowed to practice their customs. During this time, many people held smaller and surreptitious potlatches, but now the custom has been more or less revived. Hospitality exchanges between Indigenous peoples help to reinforce their religious worldview and to see the world between the living and the dead as an integrated one, in which food and gifts serve as currency in both this world and the next.

Afterlife imaginaries and their constructions give way to religious remembrance rituals that serve to reinforce the religious worldview. Remembrance rituals serve to remember and honor the dead, make sense out of loss, and to re-integrate and re-structure a community without the deceased. Through regular liturgical observances, ritualized hospitality exchanges, and calendrical ceremonies, afterlives take shape and are perpetuated after death. In Chapter 7, we will turn to the ways in which technology helps and hinders these afterlives, and question how and whether technology helps in grief management.

REFERENCES

Afikul Islam, Maulana. "Al Barzakh—the realm after death in Islam." *IslamicInformation.net* 24 (2008), last accessed March 20, 2022.

Barker, Kenneth L., Mark L. Strauss, Jeannine K. Brown, Craig L. Blomberg, and Michael Williams, eds. *NIV Study Bible*. Grand Rapids, MI: Zondervan, 2020.

Islamic Burial. "Prayers: Dua's and prayers for before, during and after the burial." http://islamicburial.co.uk/public_html/index.php/prayers-and-duas/, last accessed May 12, 2022.

Sullivan, Martha Adams. "May the circle be unbroken: The African-American experience of death, dying and spirituality." In Joan K. Parry and Angela Shen Ryan, eds, *A Cross-Cultural Look at Death, Dying, and Religion*, Chicago, IL: Nelson-Hall, 1995.

United States Conference of Catholic Bishops. n.d. "Prayers for Death and Dying." https://www.usccb.org/prayers/prayers-death-and-dying, last accessed May 12, 2022.

Walter, Tony. "Communicating with the Dead," In C. Bryant, and D. Peck, eds, *Death and the Human Experience*, Newbury Park, CA: Sage, 2009.

FOR FURTHER READING

Bracken, Christopher. *The Potlatch Papers: A Colonial Case History*. Chicago, IL: University of Chicago Press, 1997.

This book is one of the best sources offering a detailed history of the potlatch and its history under colonialism.

Falkenhain, Marc, and Paul J. Handal. "Religion, death attitudes, and belief in afterlife in the elderly: Untangling the relationships." *Journal of Religion and Health* 42, no. 1 (2003): 67–76.

This study investigated the relationship between religion, belief in an afterlife, and death attitudes (death anxiety and death acceptance) in an elderly population, finding that strong afterlife constructs correlated to lower death anxiety.

Moreman, Christopher M. *Beyond the Threshold: Afterlife Beliefs and Experiences in World Religions*. Lanham, MD: Rowman & Littlefield, 2017.

This book outlines the roles that afterlife beliefs and religious experience play in death, dying, and grief, starting from ancient Mesopotamia to the contemporary world today.

Thorson, James A. "Afterlife constructs, death anxiety, and life reviewing: The importance of religion as a moderating variable." *Journal of Psychology and Theology* 19, no. 3 (1991): 278–284.

This article examines death anxiety of individuals and its relationship to church attendance, self-rating of religiosity, and afterlife concerns, and found that afterlife conceptions have higher correlations with death anxiety than did either self-rated religiosity or frequency of church-going.

Thrane, Susan. "Hindu end of life: Death, dying, suffering, and karma." *Journal of Hospice and Palliative Nursing* 12, no. 6 (2010): 337–342.

This brief article is a succinct summary of Hindu end of life customs.

Wilson, Joseph AP. "North American indigenous afterlife beliefs." In *The Routledge Companion to Death and Dying*, pp. 184–193. Milton Park, UK: Routledge, 2017.

This short chapter covers North American indigenous afterlife beliefs.

TECHNOLOGICAL AFTERLIVES

INTRODUCTION

In Chapters 5 and 6, we examined religious afterlives and their intersections with mourning and bereavement customs. This chapter examines the shifting landscape of dying, disposal, grief, and afterlife beliefs and how technological developments may influence that landscape. This chapter also questions the viability of religious observances regarding the dead in the face of these new technologies, examining how these new ways of interacting with the dead may either strengthen or minimize religiosity. From post-mortem photography to smartphones to virtual and augmented reality, new technologies help to create new rituals where both real life and online communities gather to mourn the dead. Technologies also allow access to communities without requiring religious affinity. In this chapter, I am interested in an analysis of the current ways in which technology is utilized in death and afterlife across cultures (as seen in Chapters 2 and 3, it varies greatly), and a thoughtful prediction of the ways in which technology might be used in our future.

Technology can be seen as primarily useful—it serves to democratize grieving by allowing access to virtual spaces that might have been difficult to access in real life. During the pandemic, for example, people were able to come together online from all over the world in a virtual space in order to grieve their loved ones and to honor them even if they were unable to gather in person. Technology brings communities together to remember the dead, allowing people to participate in sacred rituals that were once limited by physical time

DOI: 10.4324/9780429025075-7

and space, yet are now accessible in the virtual realm. In Singapore, under strict COVID-19 restrictions, Buddhist temples offered virtual prayers for the dead that were livestreamed on Facebook for the families and friends of the dead. In this way, families were able to access religious rituals for the deceased even though they were unable to gather in person. Technology, and the broader access to the Internet through both computers and smartphones, grants access to wider participation in memorialization and remembrance rituals across class, gender, religion, and geographic location.

But there are also negative ways in which technology and death intersect. For example, the trend in Japan in the early 2000s of anonymous group suicide, in which people met in chatrooms in order to die together as a group (Samuels, 2007), choosing a time and place for multitudes of strangers to collectively die by suicide so they wouldn't die alone. And although this particular example is from 2007, group suicides in Japan continue to be a highly problematic issue. Another example might be the recently developed "euthanasia" machines (SARCO) that allow a person to die rapidly and (relatively) painlessly (Cubertson, 2018). While the machines offer a relatively painless avenue to death, the technological ease of the machines don't require a moral or ethical examination of one's choice to die. Technological advances in this case are not always positive, and other more common technological issues, such as online bullying, catfishing, or doxing, occasionally spill over into the online grief world, causing even more trauma to already difficult grieving experiences. The parents of the Newtown children who were gunned down in an elementary school shooting, for example, were accused of making up their children's deaths, and had their addresses published online, leading to physical harassment and threats that moved from the online world into their physical one, forcing many of the grieving families to move and keep their identities secret. The online world is not always one that makes death and grief an easier experience.

DIGITAL MEMORIALS[1]

Death is an inherently social experience, and the way in which death is understood and grieved is, in part, socially and culturally constructed and managed (Christensen and Willerslev 2013, p. 5).

Digital memorials are online spaces created to remember and honor the dead, and serve the dual aim of making sense of death and perpetuating bonds with the dead. Because of their primarily public nature, the study of digital memorials offers a unique opportunity to examine mourning responses to death. Traditional grieving patterns focus on sense-making, which includes understanding, processing, and remembering the dead through thinking about the death, positing questions about the death, and offering lamentations about the dead. These various aspects reflect an attempt to come to a gradual acceptance of a death and help the bereaved navigate a world without the deceased. Digital memorials offer one approach to sense-making following a death, providing a forum through which to grieve and understand the death, while renegotiating the world of the living without the deceased. However, digital memorials also seem to have an additional function in which the dead are gradually reinserted into the realm of the living in such a way that the deceased participates in the realm of the living in a way that accommodates their new status as a dead person. Ranging from personal postings written to the deceased themselves to re-orienting the living to a world in which the deceased are no longer present and responsive, memorialization online primarily serves to assist with the bereavement process and help the living live in a world without the dead (Christensen and Gotved 2015).

When digital memorials started, they generally fit one of three categories: **Funeral industry-driven memorial sites** such as online obituaries and guest books, **spontaneous memorials** emerging out of Social Network Sites (SNS) such as Facebook, Twitter, Pinterest, Discord, and Instagram, and **Online Support Network (OSN) memorial websites** intentionally started as support networks for the bereaved. A last category of digital memorial, the digital avatar, is expanding in popularity, but is still fairly new in both technology and usage. The **digital avatar** is a programmable likeness that someone creates and stores on a website that records the voice, face, gestures, and expressions of a person, and then leaves for one's family and friends to interact with online after one has died. Thus far there is limited research on the digital avatar's utilization and emphasis on the grieving process as the software is still in an early development stage, but is beginning to be more widely available (see the For Further Reading section at the end of this chapter).

FUNERAL INDUSTRY DIGITAL MEMORIALS

Funeral companies leading the trend of offering Internet memorials have traditionally been large industry franchises, with companies such as Service Corporation International (one of the largest funeral home companies in the United States, with approximately 13% of the funeral industry market revenue in North America, generating approximately $2.05 billion dollars in 2020 alone) offering Internet memorialization packages with software platform support at the national level. Before the pandemic, older and smaller funeral establishments generally did not offer Internet services as part of their funeral package, though as companies struggled to survive during the pandemic, this number dramatically shifted. **Funeral industry memorial sites** function as online guestbooks or repositories for obituaries, with little changing in the shift from the on-site funeral to an online guestbook. The funeral industry digital memorials usually list the funeral services held at a particular funeral home over the course of a month or two (after which they are permanently and digitally archived). Once the visitor clicks on the deceased's name, she is brought to the deceased individual's site, where an obituary of the deceased, along with any videos and photos that the family and friends have chosen to upload, is generally available. The obituary, and frequently the photos selected to accompany the obituary narrative, are most often the same as those published in the newspaper following the person's death.

Funeral home memorial websites do not differ much from the formal memorialization process already in place, constructing a narrative arc of the deceased person's life (generally told in the third person) and usually listing the primary relations of the deceased. In this way, the funeral home memorial tends to privilege the natal family of the deceased as one of primary importance, constructing the biographical narrative in a factual manner, rather than an affective one. The obituary narrates the linear timeline of a person's life, including biographical data such as birthplace, death place, and names and ages of remaining family, even though the deceased may or may not have remained close with her biological family.

Additionally, the obituary constructs a narrative based on fact, yet often separated from motive or interpretation. The primary aim of the obituary is to notify the public of the death, to re-map the deceased person's place into the past, and to notify the public of the bereaved family's changed grieving status.

One of the initially touted benefits of the funeral industry memorial page is that it presents a feasible way to allow grievers to be present regardless of proximity or distance, and to this aim, many of these sites also permit and encourage the lighting of virtual candles, the giving of virtual gifts such as flowers and teddy bears, and the writing of messages to the deceased. In this way, the virtual memorial site replicates the funeral home experience of bringing gifts to the casket, and/or lighting candles in honor of the deceased. That being said, more informal language and the tendency to use the second person present tense when speaking to the deceased (e.g., "I miss you so much Jan! May you rest in peace") seems to have gradually made its way onto the virtual guest books of the online funeral home sites, and in this way the shifting language and practices brought about by mourning on SNS (as discussed below) is transforming the more formalized practices of the funeral home. Additionally, funeral homes are now making more use of visual rhetoric as part of their services, employing video funeral services as a way to increase distance participation and visitation, and allowing visitors to their sites to occasionally upload their own pictures and videos to the funeral home website.

When examining the funeral industry digital memorials, it is important to note their monetary function. Just as SNS have incorporated ads and shopping into their news feeds, funeral homes have also made good use of the possibilities of a virtual marketplace, most often providing links to florists and other funeral-appropriate gift shops in return for fee-based advertising space. Ad space on sites is generally determined by the number of page views or visitors to the site per month, so funeral homes can easily add to their overall revenue, in addition to increasing the functionality of their websites, by offering ad space to services and products related to the funeral. Visitors to funeral websites can offer free virtual candles and teddy bears to the deceased, in addition to purchasing real flowers and tangible gifts to give at the funeral ceremony. In addition, monetary donations, particularly when the family of the deceased has asked for contributions to a particular charity in memory of the deceased, are also an option on these funeral industry digital memorials. Links to a charity's webpage can be posted on the memorial site, and friends and family of the deceased can simply click on the link and offer a donation in addition to or in lieu of other monetary gifts. These monetary donations range widely: Donations utilized to offset medical and funeral expenses, donations to favorite charities of the deceased, monetary purchases of gifts to be offered at the funeral home ceremony itself, and finally, monetary contributions given to the family of the deceased. This is not just in the United States; in China, funeral home websites have dramatically increased their web traffic as accessibility has grown. The largest funeral provider in China, the Fu Shou Yuan group, has been providing online services and "cloud tomb sweeping" for over a decade, but since the COVID pandemic, has demonstrated a 60% increase in website visits. More recent developments in the funeral industry offer interactive bar codes and/or Internet links that can be printed on the funeral program, providing access to a playlist, a virtual memorial, or even a running slideshow that one can take home following a funeral and access later via smartphone or personal computer. These bar codes and links to online memorials function as a bridge between the physical and virtual realms.

QR CODES AND VIRTUAL MEMORIALIZATION

In addition to utilizing the QR code for memorialization, the Chinese funeral industry has also found a unique solution to the religious "problem" of annual offerings and prayers for the dead at the Qing Ming festival through QR code memorials. While publicly discounting and dismissing the problems caused by the "sentimental and feudalistic" need for mourners to make offerings to, for, and on behalf of the deceased, nevertheless, the Chinese government (which owns, operates, and manages all cemeteries in China) has created a unique solution that acknowledges and allows for a religious function on behalf of the mourners. The virtual memorials accessed by the QR codes allow the bereaved to make offerings, burn candles, and virtually clean the grave from afar, allowing them to virtually visit and care for the dead from the comfort of their own phone. The Chinese government utilizes QR codes and Internet memorials to reduce the negative effects of religiosity—namely the occupation of a physical space and foot traffic to visit the graves. In this way, the Chinese government is able to reduce the negative side effects of religious observance—but it remains to be seen how the transference of the observance from the physical realm to a virtual one will affect the Chinese religious experience.

Similarly, in Hong Kong, where land burial is frequently discouraged, sea reef burial is viewed as much more environmentally friendly, cheaper, and more economical (Kong, 2012); along with this shift, smartphone applications allow grieving relatives to leave virtual offerings, prayers, light candles, etc., at the ocean gravesite. These phone applications allow mourners to grieve in real time while performing religious rituals through technology in ways that seem new, but yet are timeless. Here, the presence of the sacred is made manifest through technology. Phone applications will soon become far more ubiquitous than website memorialization, as they are widely used, and generally more accessible than even computers.

SOCIAL NETWORK MEMORIALS

Social Network memorials include memorials posted (usually spontaneously) on SNS such as Instagram, Facebook, Twitter, Discord, and Pinterest. Although traditional bereavement customs and language on SNS originally emerged spontaneously, over time particular grieving rituals seem to have been almost universally adopted by those on these sites. These customs generally include: (1) the posting of a photo of the bereaved with the deceased, (2) the posting of a message or messages to the deceased on his/her SNS, and (3) regular visits to the page or feed of the deceased on particular holidays, such as the birthday of the deceased or on the anniversary of the person's death (Cann, 2014, pp. 105–131). While there are those who do not use social media, the online mourning customs emerging today are in fact developing a syntax of mourning that will continue to be used for years to come (e.g., exclamatory statements, the use of emojis in place of words, visual rhetoric or pictures in place of written rhetoric, etc.).

That being said, all of these online rituals of grief are subject to platform constraints, and these parameters then shift the ways in which people express and understand their grief, affecting the real-life mourning processes.

On SNS, mourners commonly post pictures of themselves with the deceased, establishing the relationship between the bereaved and the deceased, and notifying the bereaved person's audience of her right to mourn. On Facebook, this is usually a changing of the profile picture, while on Instagram, it is often the posting to the Instagram feed of the mourner and deceased together (while still alive), for the purpose of identifying to one's social network that one is grieving. The practice of posting a picture of oneself with the deceased originally was a picture of the poster and the deceased when they were still living, as a mark that they knew the deceased and therefore had a right to mourn. This has more recently shifted, however, especially on image-driven sites with little to no accompanying written messages (such as Instagram or Twitter) to pictures of the poster at the funeral itself. About ten years ago, this practice initially led to the posting of "funeral selfies"—most often pictures of oneself crying or in funeral clothes, though occasionally the posting of oneself with the corpse itself. In this way, the Funeral Selfie is not unlike nineteenth century post-mortem photography, and may be as much a social commentary on innovative uses of new technologies as it is on mourning. On Instagram or Twitter, the poster often will post a picture of himself with the deceased while they were still alive and/or write a message to the dead, such as "RIP Christopher! You will be missed!" This short message (fitting the constraints of the SNS platform) allows for followers to see at once that the poster is grieving.

The practice of writing directly to the deceased is not a *new* practice per se, but rather the previously private conversations that people had with the dead (in their heads, written in journals or diaries, and at the tombstone) are now written on public social media platforms and occur on public online platforms with an audience. In other words, what is new about these postings is the fact that they are occurring in public spaces, not that they are occurring at all. The functional purpose of these postings to the deceased is to re-negotiate the world without the deceased, and they represent a desire on behalf of the living to find a way to re-insert the deceased, in their new status, into the realm of the living. By posting one's thoughts and feelings to the deceased, the mourner is also learning to re-negotiate their new relationship. The deceased will never respond to the bereaved, and yet, the virtual network provides a space, both public and universally accessible, in which to remember and memorialize. The last notable custom on digital SNS memorials is the trend to visit and revisit the pages on birthdays, death anniversaries, and in the first few months following the death. Continuing Bonds Theory (previously discussed in Chapter 4) essentially espouses the notion that people use social media to continue their relationships with the dead, as one way in which they can integrate their new bonds with the dead as deceased individuals. In this way, grievers can move forward with the dead reintegrated into their lives (Klass, Silverman, & Nickman 2014) in such a way that the bereaved are able to adjust to their loss while reorienting their lives in their new status as grievers. Grieving then is seen as an ongoing process, rather than a one-time event (Christensen and Gotved, 2015). Social media thus can give some grievers a way to "stay in touch with the dead" that allows them to simultaneously function in the real world without the deceased.

The irony of the utilization of SNS memorials to grieve the deceased, however, is that many people find it disruptive and disturbing when, for example, they log into their Facebook or twitter account and are confronted with pictures or messages of their friends and family with the deceased. While some users of SNS find posting their grief online to be a soothing practice, others are disturbed by the fact that they are interrupted by grief while utilizing SNS, particularly when many of these messages are deeply personal, upsetting, and may be accompanied by photos of the deceased. Those that prefer to manage their grief quietly and privately may not be comfortable with the blatant social nature of digital memorials. Finally, traditional hierarchies of mourning are often not replicated in SNS memorials, as families, for example, may not have the exclusive or primary position in online bereavement. Some may find this loss of recognition as the primary griever disturbing, rather than comforting (Cann 2014, pp. 120–121).

ONLINE SUPPORT NETWORK MEMORIALS

Online Support Network memorials have undergone little change since their initial emergence on the web in the late 1990s, largely continuing to function as support (either emotional or financial) for the bereaved and providing resources and support for mourners who generally share something in common. Usually these sites center around a shared type of loss, such as the loss of a child or a teen, or the death of a loved one to a commonly experienced disease or circumstance, such as suicide, cancer, or drunk driving. These sites function differently from the guestbook of funeral home memorial sites in that they also serve to inform, educate, raise financial capital, and provide resources to the bereaved, in addition to serving as memorials. Thus, the OSN memorial operates on several levels, utilizing the memorial format to capitalize resources and generate social networks. OSN memorials are often geared toward a community built only on shared experience, but not of affinity, class, or kinship relations. These different types of OSN memorials both serve to provide resources that might not otherwise be provided to the bereaved, and yet the audiences are specifically geared toward a shared experience of death. The audience of OSN memorials is thus quite different than either funeral industry or SNS digital memorials in that the OSN memorials function as communal mourning and grieving sites, as well as political and educational platforms. Thus, while SNS digital memorials function to provide an audience for highly individualized and stylized grieving, OSN memorials have a social networking purpose beyond the individual deceased persons.

PORTABLE MEMORIALIZATION: THE SMARTPHONE

With the advent of smartphone usage, and its nearly ubiquitous saturation of the market throughout the industrialized world, memorialization is also moving into smartphone applications, and in the next five years, this promises to be the most rapidly growing sector of growth in the memorialization realm. Funeral companies who are not able to move into the phone application realm may soon find themselves being viewed as outdated and outmoded, as most people no longer rely solely on websites or SNS to conduct their grief or memorialization. Smartphones are easily accessible, portable, and in many countries, considered absolutely essential to everyday life, so it is little surprise that thanatological phone applications will be widely available. New phone applications include applications like Chptr, which is a new phone application (https://www.chptr.com/) that allows users to collate and share their photos, songs, videos, and memories of a deceased person on a phone application memorial that is regularly updated. The application then notifies users of new material, while simultaneously creating communities around the deceased, and giving them a personal grief community with group chat and sharing. The functionality of phone applications like this allows real-time updates and shareability functions that are more private than website support groups because they require personal invitations in order to join, thus preventing Internet trolling or lurking. While there have been grief support phone applications for a few years, which have been met with mixed success, memorialization applications promise to be more successful because they mix the functionality of online memorializing with the support of small communities.

DIGITAL AVATARS

Not in the category of digital memorials, but serving a similar function, are **digital avatars**, which will continue to grow in popularity as the software improves and people become more comfortable with their use. By uploading biographical data and organizing it into recognizable and mappable information, companies such as Lifenaut (https://www.lifenaut.com/) claim to be able to create a digital likeness with which one can interact. While these digital avatars are currently seen as experimental, some companies are intentionally curating digital information in order to "be remembered forever." Users interacting with the avatars are prompted to type in a question or a comment to which the digital avatar will respond based on all the catalogued information. Because the person creates the avatar with pictures, video, and voice, if there is enough information, the computer-generated avatar responds to the typed question based on what the person *would have* said. However, one needs to spend a fair amount of time interacting with one's avatar in order for the avatar to reach any kind of true likeness to one's real-life self; otherwise, the results may in fact be more frustrating than comforting. Obviously, the avatars that have been the most intentionally mapped and curated will be the most accurate digital representations of the person creating them. This technology is more commonly known as **transhumanism**, which is the idea that technology and scientific advancement can be used to circumvent human limitations such as sickness, suffering, and death itself. Eventually, transhumanists hope to one day merge the online data files of a person with their bio-file, storing a person's DNA in cold storage to one day be merged with their computer-generated presence in order to be resurrected not only online, but in real life too. While some may feel that this technology is too futuristic, there are several companies actively working to make this a reality. Sequencing the genome should make it easier to create copies of ourselves for virtual (and in some ways, very real) afterlives.

Though at first glance, one might be able to utilize the continuing bonds theory discussed earlier as one way to point to a healthy utilization of interaction with the digital avatar in the grieving process, the difference is that the avatar functions in a more personal space so the griever is not interacting with the dead in a space in which all acknowledge the death of the deceased. Additionally, while the other three categories of digital memorials—funeral industry, SNS, and OSN memorials—all seem to provide a positive outlet and location in which to conduct the bereavement process, digital avatars serve to offer an entirely different type of afterlife that is not religious, but technological. Digital avatars, however, may not actually relocate the deceased as much as deny them their place as the dead. Because the technology is so new, however, it remains to be seen whether these avatars are helpful or harmful in the bereavement process. Those who are skeptical of digital avatars as helpful in mourning may find themselves sounding like those who were equally skeptical of post-mortem photography or filmmaking, but this remains one of the more interesting areas to watch in terms of future thanatechnologies.

GAMING

One of the often overlooked areas of technological afterlives is in gaming. Because virtual gaming has become so popular, many people have formed online communities with other gamers, and have turned to those same communities to manage their feelings around death, dying, and grief online. Some players have created virtual cemeteries where they "bury" and remember particular characters who have died, while others will have online memorial ceremonies for real-life players who have died, but were active in the gaming world. This phenomena shouldn't be discounted since many people spend much of their time online, and these communities are often important sources of support and friendship to gamers. In addition to people utilizing existing game worlds to create online cemeteries and memorialization rituals, there are also games centered around the themes of dying, death, or grief that help players manage their own feelings around these events. One example is a PC game called *Before Your Eyes* (https://www.beforeyoureyesgame.com/), a 2021 adventure game developed by GoodbyeWorld Games and published by Skybound Games. It was released on Microsoft Windows on April 8, 2021, and is a game from the perspective of someone recently deceased on their way to the afterlife. The player's blinks, measured through one's webcam, affect the rate at which one moves through their memories. It came out within the past year, and was fairly popular. The game is unusual because it forces the player to think about their own life and to come to terms with their mortality, asking them to think about the memories that make their own life meaningful.

Another game with a theme centered on death, dying, and grief is *That Dragon, Cancer*, released in 2016 by Numinous games. This game is an autobiographical game that narrates a story based on the Greens' experience of raising their son Joel, who was diagnosed with terminal cancer at twelve months old. Though only given a short time to live, Joel survived for four more years before dying in March 2014. The player experiences the low and high moments of this period in the Greens' lives in the style of a point-and-click adventure game, immersing the player in the situation from their perspective. While playing the game, the player quickly comes to realize that no matter what she does, she cannot change the outcome of her son dying, and ultimately, the game seems to emphasize the point that death and grief are universal. Gamers who play the game realize the heartbreak of having a child who is dying, while also experiencing a sense that all suffer grief when someone dies, and that they are ultimately not alone in their experience of grief. Gaming is one of the more unique areas where technology and death intersect, and like phone applications, an area to keep watching as new ways of thinking about death and the afterlife emerge.

OTHER MEDIA

Along with gaming, other media also deal with the themes of death, dying, and grief. In South Korea, a TV show titled "Meeting You" made by South Korean broadcaster MBC, utilized virtual reality (VR) technology to resurrect a woman's daughter who had died at age seven ("Bringing the dead back to life: South Korean VR documentary 'Meeting You'"). In order to create the VR likeness, the TV show used a digital avatar modeled upon a child actor, and then overlaid the actor with the mother's photos and memories of her deceased child. The child's mother then interacted with her VR child, telling her things she felt unable to tell her real child who died years before. The show is heartbreaking, and yet, the family of the deceased little girl claims that the experience was helpful for them to be better able to process her death. Televisions shows, movies, and books have been addressing the issue of death, dying, and grief for years, but "Meeting You" is particularly unusual in its intersection of both a real life death experience and VR.

Thanatechnologies are expanding rapidly, and as advances in technology continue to grow, this will be one of the most interesting areas to watch. All areas of technology are grappling with the implications of real life dying, death, and grief, from podcasts to the metaverse. Podcasts such as *Crime Junkies* and other true crime podcasts help to shine a spotlight on traumatic deaths and what we can do to advocate for justice and resolution. The metaverse with its virtual land has already established virtual cemeteries with virtual memorials sold as NFTs (or non-fungible-tokens) held in one's cryptocurrency wallet as a tradeable currency. Just as life makes these virtual worlds and realities possible, virtual death also creates virtual afterlives and memorials, with virtual spaces to grieve and remember. Now it is possible to live not just religious afterlives, but technological ones.

CONCLUSION

Chapters 5 and 6 have demonstrated various ways of dealing with death after life—either through grief, religious constructs of an afterlife, or various religious rituals and customs observed and practiced to help make sense of loss after death. The question remains whether technology is a useful tool that increases the viability of religious observances regarding the dead or whether it becomes a tool that allows people to circumvent religious tradition and create their own, more personalized rituals. In other words, thanatechnologies may either strengthen or minimize religiosity. Because so many software platforms are governed and constrained by their own parameters (the 280 character tweet or @mentions for example), it will be interesting to watch as technological constraints spill over into religion and vice versa.

NOTE

1 Some parts of this section have been previously published in Candi K. Cann, "Digital memorials" in *The Routledge Companion to Death and Dying*, pp. 307–316. Routledge, 2017.

REFERENCES

"Bringing the dead back to life: South Korean VR documentary 'Meeting You,'" April 8, 2020, YouTube video, https://www.youtube.com/watch?v=7RF44KDzyAc (last accessed May 10, 2022) to view the original episode with English subtitles.

Cann, Candi K. *Virtual Afterlives: Grieving the Dead in the Twenty-First Century*. Lexington, KY: University Press of Kentucky, 2014.

Christensen, Dorthe Refslund, and Rane Willerslev, eds. Taming Time, Timing Death: Social Technologies and Ritual. *Studies in Death, Materiality and Time*, Volume 1. Burlington, VT: Ashgate, 2013.

Christensen, Dorthe Refslund, and Stine Gotved. "Online memorial culture: An introduction." *New Review of Hypermedia and Multimedia* 21, no. 1–2 (2015): 1–9.

Cubertson, Anthony. "Suicide Machine that could be controlled by the blink of an eye sparks euthanasia debate," *The Independent*, 17 April, 2018. https://www.independent.co.uk/tech/suicide-machine-assisted-dying-euthanasia-debate-ukclinicsarco-nitschke-a8307741.html, last accessed May 10, 2022.

Klass, Dennis, Phyllis R. Silverman, and Steven Nickman. *Continuing Bonds: New Understandings of Grief*. Milton Park, UK: Taylor & Francis, 2014.

Kong, Lily. "No place, new places: Death and its rituals in urban Asia." *Urban Studies* 49, no. 2 (2012): 415–433.

Samuels, David. "Let's Die Together," *The Atlantic*, May, 2007, https://www.theatlantic.com/magazine/archive/2007/05/let-s-die-together/305776/, last accessed May 9, 2022.

FOR FURTHER READING

Transhumanism

Ahmad, Muhammad. "After Death: Big Data and the Promise of Resurrection by Proxy," 07-12-:397–408. CHI EA '16. ACM, 2016.

This paper examines the ramifications of resurrecting people through the data capture online in their lifetimes, and asks questions about possible ethical implications.

Bassett, Debra. "Ctrl+Alt+Delete: The changing landscape of the uncanny valley and the fear of second loss." *Current Psychology*, 2018: 1–9. https://doi.org/10.1007/s12144-018-0006-5.

Using qualitative methods, this article examines how internet afterlife might affect how people grieve.

Virtual grief

Cann, Candi K. *Virtual Afterlives: Grieving the Dead in the Twenty-first Century*. Lexington, Kentucky: University Press of Kentucky, 2014.

This book examines the rise of online memorialization, tying it to a historical trend of DIY memorialization as contemporary culture minimized grief and corporate culture reduced the grieving time.

Cann, Candi K., "Pocket Memorials: Digital Death and the Smartphone." *Oxford Handbook of Digital Religion*, Oxford, England: Oxford University Press, forthcoming 2022.

A brief overview of the way smartphones have impacted death and grief.

Christensen, Dorthe Refslund, and Stine Gotved. "Online memorial culture: An introduction." *New Review of Hypermedia and Multimedia* 21, no. 1–2 (April 3, 2015): 1–9.

An introduction to the field up to the point of publication.

Gibbs, Martin, James Meese, Michael Arnold, Bjorn Nansen, and Marcus Carter. "#Funeral and Instagram: Death, Social Media, and Platform Vernacular." *Information, Communication and Society* 18, no. 3 (2015): 255–268.

This paper argues that platform vernaculars (including online mourning) are shaped through the logics of architecture and use.

Moreman, Christopher M., and A. David Lewis. *Digital Death: Mortality and Beyond in the Online Age.* Westport, CT: ABC-CLIO, LLC, 2014.

Drawing from a range of academic perspectives, this book studies ways in which death, dying, and memorialization appear in and are influenced by digital technology.

Walter, Tony. "New mourners, old mourners: Online memorial culture as a chapter in the history of mourning." *New Review of Hypermedia and Multimedia* 21, no. 1–2 (2015): 10–24. https://doi.org/10.1080/13614568.2014.983555.

This article examines how online mourning is different from offline mourning.

CONCLUSION

SECULAR AFTERLIVES

When writing about religious and technological afterlives, some people might be tempted to discount the religious nature of technological afterlives, but these can be viewed as religious responses in so far as they address religious questions of meaning and loss. Sam Keen's definition of religion as "ultimate answers to ultimate questions" allows these technological afterlives to operate in the religious sphere and be taken seriously as claims on ultimate meaning. There are some religious points of view not covered in *Death and Religion: The Basics,* and this book does not claim to be an exhaustive examination of the many religions around the world, but these absences should be noted. Among those missing are the "nones," or those who claim no religious affiliation, and atheists, both of whom, I would argue, offer their own religious responses to religious questions. Around the globe, the "nones" account for 16% of the world's population, and in the United States, approximately 20–30% of all people identity as a member of the "nones," or as having no religious affiliation in particular. Some scholars prefer the term "unchurched" for this group, arguing that this group generally claims a spiritual belief but do not actively practice or belong to a religious affiliation. In fact, the Pew Research Center found that in 2017, 72% of those who identified as "none" also claimed a belief in a higher spiritual power (Fahmey, 2018). Thus, a lack of belonging does not necessarily preclude a lack of belief. This can make including this population somewhat difficult in studies of religion, but it is important that they be mentioned

DOI: 10.4324/9780429025075-8

since they represent a fairly significant proportion of society. The most important characteristic for our purposes is noting that this group is increasingly growing and represents a fairly substantial part of the contemporary American landscape. This also might be why the trend toward DIY memorialization is growing as well, since nearly one-fifth of all Americans do not ascribe to a particular religious faith or practice.

MARGINAL AFTERLIVES: GHOSTS, ZOMBIES, AND MONSTERS

Other afterlives worth mentioning are those that migrate to popular culture and folklore—ghosts, zombies, and monsters are found throughout the world in various cultures and throughout time. Ghosts often represent social anxieties and ghost stories emerge in every cultural context, with ghosts frequently representing people who have died unsanctioned deaths that have no place in everyday life. Most often, ghost stories tell the story of someone who died a tragic death, or died in a way that is not socially sanctioned, and cannot be redeemed through ritual or religious purification. Ghosts are most often people who died from murder, suicide, or untimely deaths, and their haunting reminds the living that the dead are important and should be remembered. Different cultures manage ghosts in different ways. In Japan, for example, aborted and miscarried fetuses are cared for in religious rituals undertaken by Buddhist priests that help manage the individual and social anxieties surrounding abortion and miscarriage. A ritual known as **mizuko kuyō**, or the water child memorial service, is performed by one or both parents as a way to appease the spirit of the fetus and to help manage the feelings of sadness, guilt, or ambivalence regarding the miscarriage or abortion. In China, ghost stories abound of women who died by suicide, and the ways in which their spirits return to haunt the living. The stories tell of vengeful spirits eager to re-enact and revisit the living with harm in revenge for their unhappy lives. While at first glance these stories seem like vengeful tales meant to scare young children, they also provide a way for women to critique a society that was and is traditionally patriarchal, providing narrative retribution in a system in which men learn that their actions do indeed have consequences, even if only later, or through the supernatural. Ghosts, though marginal in their afterlives, matter to the living and their stories reveal the social anxieties of a society, while also providing a voice to those who might be marginalized in life.

Zombies, or the living dead, are another example of the importance of marginal afterlives, and another cultural phenomenon found around the world. Zombies are the dead who are both living and dead—they have lost their agency, have no will, or rational thought and behavior, and yet, their corpses are often controlled and manipulated for evil intent, and thrive by eating the brains of the living. Like ghosts, stories of zombies reveal social and cultural anxieties surrounding corpses that come back to life, yet lack our rational control. Relatively new in comparison to their ghostly counterparts (they seem to have emerged in the 1800s around or near the industrial revolution), zombies may reflect anxieties around capitalism, as bodies relegated to do work without our consent. In some ways, zombies reflect our fears surrounding bodies without souls and dualistic views of the self. Zombies are in short what bodies could become without the soul to inhabit it. In this way, zombies represent the worst possibility of an afterlife.

Finally, **monsters** are the third category of marginal afterlives, with figures such as Frankenstein representing another form of corrupted afterlife in the margins. When Mary Shelley wrote her seminal work, *Frankenstein*, modern medicine was still emerging, and anatomy and dissection still a developing science. Because doctors needed practice and familiarity with the human body, it was not uncommon for them to pay for indigent corpses from the graveyard; this led to a rampant trafficking of corpses often procured by illegal and questionable means. Frankenstein thus represents the dead, now disfigured and piecemeal, corpse, cementing the genre of monsters for years to come. Today's monsters are often cyborg humans—part human and part robot—but still representing the anxieties regarding self and body and questioning the ways in which technological and medical advances might change our souls. Contemporary monster stories center on tales of medical nightmares—donated organs that remember their past lives or pollute us with corrupt souls, technological implants that taint our essential self, or fleshly bodies ruined by perverted clones that somehow replicate only our appearance, at the expense of soul. Monsters interrogate the soul/body dualism found in Platonic notions of self and inherited by Christianity. Monsters, while marginal, reveal the questions and concerns we have about the world and its future.

In *Death and Religion: The Basics*, we have examined the concept of the "good death," and how the idea of a "good death" is shaped by our cultural and religious contexts. Often a good death is a death that is defined by living well—no matter what that might like in different countries or cultures—and in the contemporary medical context, dying well often means having some agency in the dying process. From there, we moved to an examination of the dying process, and the ways in which religious traditions might affect or influence how individuals die. Some religions prohibit pain relievers, or forbid organ donation, while other religions encourage palliative care and/or life extension at all costs. Understanding religious and cultural context in the dying process can help foster dialogue and create meaning in a person's dying days, and assist medical practitioners, social workers, and chaplains in better caring for patients and their families. Then, we studied the definition of death, itself, examining the ways that the understanding of death shifts with available medical technologies. Next, the book considered various forms of disposition, and interrogated the ways in which religious imaginaries of the afterlife might inform choices of disposal once a person has died. It was not merely religious views that impacted disposition, but sometimes, it was the other way around. We found that issues such as cost, land shortages, environmental concerns, and technological advances also impacted religious views on disposition, and that the tension between religiosity and everyday concerns was ongoing and reciprocal.

We then turned towards an examination of grief, mourning, and bereavement. First, we learned about the study of grief theory itself, before moving to an investigation of the various religions and the ways they create a social grammar of mourning that accompanies private and individual grief. We found that regular religious observances and calendrical rituals embedding mourning customs allow for a social structure of grief expression across religious traditions. While there was variance across traditions, almost all of the religious rituals contained a beginning and an end of one's mourning, which then segued into the larger religious calendar and a return to the community for regular and recurrent remembrance.

Then, we moved from the religious to the technological—and questioned the ways in which technology both aids and hinders the expression of grief, religious, or non-religious. Finally, we briefly considered secular ways of grappling with death, and the ways in which technology and secularism might intersect to reflect contemporary anxieties that morph into stories of ghosts, zombies, and monsters. Even marginal afterlives, then, like religious afterlives, reveal as much about life as they do about death, and the ways in which we envision ourselves and our relation to the world around us.

REFERENCES

Fahmey, Dalia. "Key findings about Americans' belief in God," Pew Research Center. April 25, 2018. https://www.pewresearch.org/fact-tank/2018/04/25/key-findings-about-americans-belief-in-god/, last accessed May 13, 2022.

FURTHER READING

Huntington, Rania. "Ghosts seeking substitutes: female suicide and repetition." *Late Imperial China* 26, no. 1 (2005): 1–40.

This article highlights the role of ghosts in revealing anxieties surrounding female suicides.

LaFleur, William R. *Liquid Life: Abortion and Buddhism in Japan*. Princeton, NJ: Princeton University Press, 1994.

This book examines the mizuko kuyō ritual in Japan and examines the development of religious rituals regarding abortion to aide in the social anxieties that arose as a result.

Luckhurst, Roger. *Zombies: A Cultural History*. London, UK: Reaktion Books, 2015.

A good history of zombies.

Marshall, Tim. *Murdering to Dissect: Grave-robbing, Frankenstein and the Anatomy Literature*. Manchester, UK: Manchester University Press, 1995.

This book highlights the anxieties surrounding bodies and medicine, through the figure of Mary Shelley's *Frankenstein*.

GLOSSARY

abhishekam: (Sanskrit) In Hinduism, and literally translated as "holy bath," this is the ritual washing of the dead with milk, ghee, honey, and yogurt meant to soften the body and purify them before cremation.

active dying: The last stage of the dying process when patients are near death.

advanced directive: Also known as a living will, this is a legal document that tells the hospital what care a patient wants and does not want, and how far to extend care, in the event that the patient becomes incapacitated.

'aha'aina waimaka: (Hawai'ian: a feast of tears) This is a commemorative anniversary feast held exactly one year following a death and is meant to both recognize the end of one year of mourning, and symbolize a new beginning.

akhirah: (Arabic) The term used to describe a belief in life after death in Islam.

alkaline hydrolysis: (Sometimes known as resomation or water cremation) Through a combination of hot water and potassium hydroxide, this process liquifies the flesh on a body, leaving only bones and ash behind.

All Souls' Day: (November 2) In Roman Catholicism, the most important regular annual service for the dead, when Catholic families gather in homes, at graves, and in churches to remember and pray for the dead.

'amakua: (Hawai'ian) In Hawai'ian religion, a deified ancestor that transforms over time to become a guardian spirit and may take the form of anything in the natural world, such as a tree, turtle, rock, or animal.

anticipatory grief: The grief that is felt before a loss, when one knows that another person or being is going to die soon; this can also describe a predictable loss, such as that for a move or a job.

antam sanskaar: (Punjabi) In Sikhism, the funeral, but literally translated as "last rite."

aquamation: (Sometimes known as resomation or water cremation) Through a combination of hot water and potassium hydroxide, this process liquifies the flesh on a body, leaving only bones and ash behind.

atman: (Sanskrit) In Hinduism, one's self, or soul; the being that migrates from body to body in reincarnation.

baptism: In Christianity, one of the seven sacraments, an initiation ritual in which the believer is blessed by holy water as a recognition that they are a member of the Christian community

barsi: (Punjabi) In Sikhism, the word for "death anniversary," used to describe the commemorative ceremony held one year after a death, and usually consisting of prayers, a community meal, and shared reflections and memories of the deceased.

barzakh: (Arabic) In Islam, the place where one awaits judgment following their death.

bereavement: A term used to designate the time during which a person experiences their grief, and describes the state of having experienced a loss.

bereavement leave: The term used by workplaces to describe an amount of time given from work to manage the affairs of the deceased, plan the funeral, and/or mourn.

bodhisattvas: In Mahayana Buddhism, divine beings that delay their own enlightenment to help others reach enlightenment.

body farms: A research facility where body decomposition can be studied in a variety of settings, and whose findings have greatly aided in the advancement of scientific research and forensic science.

Bon Odori: (盆踊り; Japanese) In Japanese Buddhism, this is a holiday celebrated annually as a time to invite the deceased to return to the earth and to offer prayers on their behalf to reach Buddhahood.

burial vault liners: Boxes (usually made of cement) in which the caskets will be placed and utilized by cemeteries in order to keep their graves level and uniform.

brain death: The irreversible cessation of brain function.

cardio–pulmonary death: The state of being when the heart and lungs cease to function, blood no longer flows, the heart stops bleeding, and lungs no longer circulate air through the circulatory system.

casket: A box or container used to bury a body; often has a hinged opening on the top, and sometimes have rails for easier carrying.

celebration of life: An informal and less structured service to honor the death of a person; usually the tone of a celebration of life is meant to remember and honor a person whereas a funeral might adhere to liturgical structures and expectations.

Cherokee Nation Remembrance Day: (March 24) The day of commemoration remembering the deaths of many who died under the forced relocation in the Trail of Tears, when the American government forcibly removed the Native Americans from their homes and relocated them a thousand miles away.

Chrismation: In Orthodox Christianity, a sacramental ceremony inducting a believer into the church when they come of age.

Christianity: The largest religion in the world, based on the teachings of Jesus Christ.

communal grief: Grief experienced by a group of people experiencing loss over a death, but perhaps in different and varying ways, with no universal or set expression of mourning.

coffin: Like a casket, a box utilized for viewing and burying a body; usually less ornate than a casket, a coffin is often wider at the top to accommodate a person's shoulders, tapering at the bottom, and has a lid without hinges.

composting: A form of disposal in which the body undergoes a process of natural organic reduction by being placed in a bin with wood chips and straw, which is then mixed with soil, and regularly turned to accelerate body decomposition.

cremains: Ashes of a deceased body (cremated remains).

columbarium: A structure for the respectful storage of remains, usually in public places such as graveyards, burial grounds, or religious places of worship.

complicated grief: Grief that keeps one in an ongoing heightened state of mourning, and is often due to a traumatic, unexpected death or because one had unresolved issues with the person who died that can never be resolved.

Confirmation: In Roman Catholicism, a sacramental ceremony inducting a believer into the church when they come of age.

Confucianism: (儒家, rujia, Chinese) An ethical system of thought based on the philosophy of Confucius, centering on social structures and living in harmony with one another. Confucianism was extremely influential in the Chinese government, and a meritocracy based on the Confucian classics ruled the Chinese government for hundreds of years.

Continuing Bonds Theory: Model of grieving developed by Klass, Silverman, and Nickman that views the ongoing attachment to the deceased as healthy and even expected.

cremation: A method of corpse disposal that relies on the burning of bodies, either in a crematorium or in an open-air pyre.

cryonics: A technique in which people who are declared legally dead are cryo-preserved in liquid nitrogen in order to preserve the body and prevent physical decay in the hopes of scientifically resurrecting them in the future.

curative care: Treatments centered on ending or curing disease, rather than the management of pain or suffering.

dakhma: See towers of silence

Daoism: (道教; daojiao, Chinese) Daoism is a nature-centered philosophy that teaches individuals to live in harmony with the world.

dead clothes: In the Cherokee tradition, the clothes a person prepares in their early adulthood for burial.

death: The termination of all biological functions in a living being.

deathbed confessions: Confessions of transgressions against God/a higher being and others as one is dying.

deathplans: A plan for the way one wishes to die, including, if applicable, the use or denial of life-sustaining equipment, the appointing of a healthcare proxy to make decisions in case one is incapacitated, the appointment of where one wishes to die, if that is an option, and an outlining of the palliative care one wishes to have administered if one is in pain.

dharma: (Sanskrit) In Buddhism, the Buddha's teachings and written scriptures

Día de los Muertos: (Spanish: Day of the Dead) The day of the dead is a Catholic holiday traditionally celebrated on November 1 and November 2 in honor of deceased loved ones in Mexico. On this day, people will clean the graveyard, make food and drink offerings, and welcome the dead back to the world of the living through altars in the home. Sugar skulls, altars, artistic depictions of skulls, and marigold flowers have become popular symbols of this holiday.

digital avatar: A programmable likeness that someone creates and stores on a website that records the voice, face, gestures, and expressions of a person.

digital memorial: An online space created to remember and honor the dead, serving the dual aim of making sense of death and perpetuating bonds with the dead.

disposition: The manner of disposal for a body once it is dead.

dying: The permanent and irreversible cessation of the biological function of life.

dying well: A death process that is somewhat manageable, and under a dying person's control, offering time for the dying person to plan for and think about their death.

dual-process model: A model of grief developed by Stroebe and Schut that suggests that the bereaved person oscillates between a loss orientation and a restoration orientation model of coping, in which a person may feel the loss of their loved one keenly, followed by periods in which they feel okay again.

Eucharist: In Christianity, one of the seven sacraments, this is the eating of blessed bread and wine with the church community, and a reenactment of Jesus' last meal with his followers.

Eightfold path: In Buddhism, these are the actions that a Buddhist is advised to take in order to best reach enlightenment.

They are right view, right aspiration, right speech, right action, right livelihood, right effort, right mindfulness, and right concentration.

embalmment: The preservation of the dead body through chemicals in order to delay the natural and visual signs of death. Many funeral homes require a body to be embalmed if there is going to be a visitation or viewing of the body; also embalming is usually required if the corpse crosses state lines.

end-of-life decisions: Your goals, preferences, and values regarding your end-of-life care, including but not limited to decisions invasive medical care, what to do should one's health rapidly decline and one is incapacitated. Some people also include funeral planning under end-of-life decisions.

excarnation: The practice of removing bodily flesh from bones through natural means, such as vultures or intentional putre-faction by exposure to the elements.

filial piety: (Chinese: xiao) The concept that there is reciprocity between family members based on age, hierarchy, and mutual respect (e.g., father to son, mother to daughter, elder brother to younger sister, etc.).

final judgment: The belief that when one dies, one's soul leaves one's body to stand before God or a higher being for a weigh-ing of one's good and bad deeds from one's lifetime.

Five K's: In Sikhism, the core five signifiers of Sikh identity, consisting of **kesh** (uncut hair), **kara** (a steel bracelet), a **kanga** (a wooden comb), **kaccha** (cotton underwear), and a **kirpan** (steel sword).

Four Noble Truths: In Buddhism, the essential Buddhist worldview. This encompasses the view that to exist is to suf-fer, that the cause of suffering is attachment to the way things are and a desire for them not to change, that the solution to suffering is to cease attachment, and that the way to cease attachment is to follow the eightfold path.

funeral: A communal ceremony regarding the final disposition of a corpse.

funeral industry memorial sites: Memorial sites attached to formal funerals held by funeral homes, and consisting of a virtual guestbook, a repository of communal memories, pictures, videos, and offerings.

Gin Salat: (Thailand) In Thai Buddhism, this holiday is the Thai version of the Chinese Hungry Ghost festival, in which the dead are honored and remembered.

good death: Changing with cultural and religious interpretation, the good death is an understanding of a live well-lived, with an optimal ending as interpreted by a person's community.

green burial: Also known as natural burial, this is a way of burying the dead in a way that minimizes environmental impact and aids in the good stewardship of natural resources and reduces carbon emissions.

grief: A reaction to the loss of a person, thing, or situation that is valued by a person.

grief theory: The study of how humans remember and mourn the dead, while making sense of the loss in their lives.

gui: (鬼, Chinese) In Chinese religion, ghosts who can, and often will, haunt the living.

Gurmantar Waheguru: (Punjabi) In Sikhism, a chant given to a new initiate that affirms their relationship with the one God. It is a mantra in which one repeats God's name (Wonderful God over and over).

gurudwara: (Punjabi) A Sikh temple.

Guru Granth Sahib: (Punjabi) The central text of Sikhism, frequently read in honor of special days, such as the blessing of a house or a funeral.

halal: (Arabic) Meaning "lawful" or "permitted," in Islam, halal food—like kosher food in Judaism—is food that has been prepared in a humane and sanitary way according to Islamic law, including a proscription against pork, alcohol, and foods containing rennet or gelatin, etc.

Holy Orders: In Christianity, the sacramental appointing of a person to a clerical position in the church.

ho'oponopono: (Hawai'ian) "Setting it right." In traditional Hawai'ian culture, the practice of ho'oponopono means to tidy up, to restore balance, and to ensure healing so that one can feel whole again.

hospice care: Solely comfort care, centered on improving the quality of the end-of-life for both patients and their families.

hospice eligibility: The requirements of a medical care system to provide a patient with hospice care. In the American healthcare system, the patient must have less than six months to live, and must be verified by two separate physicians.

hospice movement: A movement founded in the United Kingdom in 1967 by Dame Cicely Saunders, and concerned with end-of-life and palliative care services.

hospital palliative care: Care provided in the hospital utilizing a specialized palliative care team trained in managing the pain, symptoms, and stress with the specific directive of alleviating pain and stress rather than curing disease/illness.

huaka'i pō: (Hawai'ian) In Hawai'i, the mythological night marchers, or dead warriors who guard sacred religious sites, and exact violent revenge on those who disrespect the land or its people.

hun: (魂, Chinese) In Chinese religion, a piece of the soul that is placed in the ancestral tablet and then honored in the family home.

icon: In Eastern Orthodoxy, icons are paintings viewed as a window into heaven, utilized as visual tools that help believers envision a holy world that translates concepts such as "heaven" into possible realities.

incorrupt corpses: Corpses that demonstrate little or no decay following their death. Incorrupt corpses are revered in the Roman Catholic and Eastern Orthodox churches as evidence that a person is in the presence of God following their death.

iluraijuaqtut: (Inuit) A ritual marking the conclusion of the five-day mourning period, when a firestone is thrown to the floor symbolizing the end of the immediate grieving period.

inhumation: Burial

integrated grief: The technical term used to describe someone who has learned how to live and function with their grief.

intercessory prayer: Prayer on behalf of a deceased person, believed to aid them in their afterlife.

intiqal: (Arabic) Literally means to pass from one to another; a transfer to the afterlife.

Jahannam: (Arabic) In Islam, hell or a place of physical and spiritual suffering.

Jannah: (Arabic) In Islam, heaven, literally translated as paradise.

Jesus Christ: one of three persons of the Christian trinity, believed by Christians to be the son of God. His teachings are recorded in the New Testament.

kaccha: (Punjabi) In Sikhism, one of the five K's, directly translated as cotton underwear. Kaccha consists of cotton breeches ending right above the knees, symbolize bodily purity, and traditionally provided protection in horseback riding.

Kaddish: (Hebrew) In Judaism, a prayer for the dead that celebrates the sanctification and power of God.

kanga: (Punjabi) In Sikhism, one of the five K's, and the name for the wooden comb traditionally carried by all Sikhs as a symbol of their bodily care and love for God's creation.

kapu: (Hawai'ian) Taboo; something that is forbidden.

kara: (Punjabi) In Sikhism, one of the Five K's, the kara is a steel bracelet worn to signify God's eternal existence and that God has neither beginning nor end. It is generally made of steel as it is not meant to be an ornamental piece of jewelry but an acknowledgement of the eternity of God.

karhah prashad: (Punjabi) In Sikhism, a traditional sweet desert made of flour, butter, sugar, and wheat, usually given as a sign of hospitality in Sikh ceremonies.

karma: (Sanskrit) Actions from one's lifetime(s) that determine one's rebirth.

keriah: (Hebrew) In Judaism, a ribbon that symbolizes the tearing of one's clothing and signifies being in a state of grieving, worn during the entire initial mourning period of Shiva.

kesh: (Punjabi) In Sikhism, one of the Five K's, kesh is simply translated as uncut hair. In Sikhism, because hair is believed to be a part of God's creation, not cutting it is viewed as submission to God's will and honoring God's creation.

kirpan: (Punjabi) In Sikhism, one of the five K's, the kirpan is a steel sword, which can be anywhere from a few inches to a few feet long, and its significance stands for fighting injustice and serving as a warrior of God for all those who are downtrodden.

kirt karna: (Punjabi) One of the three duties of a Sikh, and literally translated as earning an honest living, this refers to the importance of working in an occupation that causes no harm and allows one to live kindly and with compassion to one's community. Working in an occupation in the tobacco and alcohol industries is strictly forbidden for Sikhs.

kirtan sohila: (Punjabi) Translated as song of praise, in Sikhism, this prayer consists of five different hymns sung at night before one retires; it is also the prayer sung as one is cremated to praise God and give one's soul to God's care.

koliva: (κόλλυβος derived from classical Greek) In Eastern Orthodoxy, a traditional dish made of boiled wheat and honey and symbolizing the cycle of life and the sweetness of heaven, often placed in the casket with the deceased, but also regularly eaten in memorial services.

Lady of the Dead: The contemporary rendering of the Aztec goddess, Mictecacihuatl, often found in contemporary Day of the Dead celebrations.

life expectancy: The estimated amount of years a person in a particular country is expected to live, often influenced by quality and access to healthcare, gender, wealth, and geographic location.

loss orientation: The state of coping with issues related to loss, and including such factors as loneliness, sadness, and helplessness.

Mahayana: One of the three schools of Buddhism, and found in China, Japan, Vietnam, and Korea, this school believes that anyone may attain enlightenment with the help of others.

makaria: (Greek) Loosely translated means the meal of blessings, this is the memorial meal held by adherents of the Eastern Orthodox church after a funeral service, in which it is common to share stories of the deceased. In the Eastern Orthodox Church, only the priest may speak in a funeral service since the focus should be on God, rather than the deceased, so this meal allows for others to eulogize the dead.

mana: (Hawai'ian) Spiritual power.

mass casualty: An event such as a school shooting, a war, pandemic, or a famine where there are many deaths at one time.

masses for the dead: (Roman Catholic) Services in which prayers for the dead are offered, particularly on significant dates following the death.

memorialization: Ways in which the living honor and remember the dead, ranging from the ritualized to the highly personal.

memory drawer: A concealed drawer in a casket that allows people to include letters, prayers, pictures, icons, prayer cards, and religious items to be buried with the deceased.

minyan: (Hebrew) In Judaism, a quorum, or the minimum number (usually ten adult males) required to hold a public prayer service.

mizuko kuyō: (水子供養, Japanese; the water child ceremony) In Japanese Buddhism, a memorial service performed by one or both parents as a way to appease the spirit of the fetus and to help manage the feelings of sadness, guilt, or ambivalence regarding the miscarriage or abortion.

moksha: (Sanskrit) In Hinduism and Buddhism, becoming one with the eternal divine and ending the cycle of samsara forever.

mortality rates: The demographic prediction of death in a population.

mourning: The way in which grief is expressed in public, which may involve particular rituals, practices, and or customs, but is usually a public expression of loss.

Mul mantar: (Punjabi) The opening verse of the Sikh scripture, the *Guru Granth Sahib*, the mul mantar consists of 12 words frequently recited, and is believed to summarize core teachings of Sikhism, but is also recited over the deceased. Literally translated, it reads, "There is one God, true name, creator, without fear, without hate, timeless in form, beyond birth, self-existent, and known by the grace of the Guru."

mukti: (Punjabi) In Sikhism, liberation, or release from the cycle of birth, death, and rebirth; in Hinduism and Buddhism, moksha.

nam japna: (Punjabi) One of the three duties of a Sikh, this means meditating on the presence of God and keeping God in one's mind at all times.

narrative grief therapy: A grief model developed by Robert Neimeyer that utilizes a variety of narrative and artistic tools to encourage grievers to reconstruct meaning in a world without their loved ones.

natural burial: Also known as green burial, this is a way of burying the dead in a way that minimizes environmental impact and aids in the good stewardship of natural resources and reduces carbon emissions.

nirvana: (Sanskrit) In Buddhism, enlightenment, leading to the cessation of the soul's participation in the endless cycle of life, death, and rebirth.

Online Support Network (OSN) memorials: Memorials in honor of people who have died in online groups gathered around particular themes or needs.

organ donation: The process of surgically removing an organ or tissue from one body to another.

Orthodox Christianity: The second largest Christian Church, Eastern Orthodoxy recognizes the Ecumenical Patriarch of Constantinople as its spiritual leader, and honors the seven sacraments, scriptures, and tradition.

palliative care: Palliative care is specialized medical care to aid in pain management and optimize a patient's quality of life.

Pan de Muerto buns: (Spanish; Mexico) Translated as "Death bread," this is a yeasty sweet bread made with flour, butter, sugar, eggs, orange peel, anise, and yeast. Along with sugar skulls, and oranges, Pan de Muerto buns are offered at the family altars along with pictures of the deceased, candles, and flowers on the Mexican Día de los Muertos holiday.

Partial brain death: Death defined by the cessation in functioning of the brainstem (rather than the entire brain).

penance: In Christianity, one of the seven sacraments, and a confession of one's misdeeds to a priest so that one may receive the forgiveness of God.

pitri: (Sanskrit; literally, father) In Hinduism, someone who has died and is considered to be a spirit or an ancestor.

pitru paksha: (Sanskrit) In Hinduism, an annual sixteen-day period that usually falls on or near the autumnal equinox, celebrated in honor of all of one's ancestors.

po: (魄, Chinese) In Chinese religion, this is the part of the soul that is buried with the body in the grave.

pollution: The belief that dead bodies are dangerous, and one can be harmed or made unclean by proximity to a dead person.

prayer cards: In Roman Catholicism, a card that contains a picture of the deceased, with their birth and death dates on one side, and a prayer of intercession for their soul on the other side, often handed out at the masses for the dead.

predestination: The belief that God/Allah/a higher power has already determined what will happen to an individual and therefore whether or not s/he will go to heaven or hell upon their death.

promession: A form of disposal that breaks down the corpse through freeze-drying, and utilizes about one-third of the energy of cremation.

purgatory: In Roman Catholicism, purgatory is a place where one's soul is sent if one's positive deeds do not necessarily outweigh the negatives ones. It is believed that the living can pray for the dead in purgatory and they can gradually have their sins reduced so that the dead may enter into heaven into the presence of God.

qing ming: (Chinese; literally clear and bright) In Chinese religion, this is tomb-sweeping day, celebrated on the fifteenth day after the spring equinox. On this day, families return to their ancestral tombs, clean burial sites, and make offerings of prayers, incense, spirit money, paper goods, wine, and food on behalf of the dead.

qingtuan: (青糰, Chinese) This is a popular food consumed on the qing ming holiday in China, and is a dark green rice cake with red bean inside.

reincarnation: In Hinduism and Buddhism, the belief that one's karma is manifested in another life cycle in order to learn the lessons left unlearned in the previous one.

restoration orientation: According to Stroebe and Schut, the state when a grieving person learns to live with, and adapt to, their loss.

resurrection: A belief that one will rise from the dead.

samsara: In Hinduism and Buddhism, the endless cycle of life, death, and rebirth.

san jiao: (三教; Chinese) In China, translated as the three teachings of Buddhism, Confucianism, and Daoism, and describing the syncretistic practices of Chinese religion.

sangha: The Buddhist clergy.

seudat havra'ah: (Hebrew) In Judaism, the first meal following a funeral, served at the home of the deceased upon returning from the cemetery and usually provided by the family, friends, and synagogue of the bereaved.

shahadah: (Arabic) In Islam, the first pillar of Islam and a profession of faith. It states, "I bear witness that there is no god but God, and that Muhammad is his messenger."

Sheol: (Hebrew) In Judaism, a place called where all the dead, both righteous and unrighteous, go after their death.

shabbat: (Hebrew) In Judaism, the holy day of rest beginning at sundown on Friday and ending at sundown on Saturday.

shen: (Chinese) In Chinese religion, a beneficent spirit of the dead, or a deity.

Shi'a: The second largest branch of Islam, comprising 10–15% of the world's total Muslim population.

shiva: (Hebrew) In Judaism, this word comes from the Hebrew word seven and correlates to the expected seven-day mourning period for all Jewish mourners.

shiva minyan: (Hebrew) In Judaism, a prayer service for the dead.

shomer: (Hebrew) In Judaism, this word means watcher, and is the person who sits with the body reading Psalms and reciting prayers on behalf of the dead.

shraddha: (Sanskrit) In Hinduism, a ceremony to pay homage to the deceased. The shraddha usually consists of gift-giving and feasting, and can last from days to weeks depending on who died and the means of the family holding the shraddha.

sky burial: (Tibetan Buddhism) A type of excarnation in which the entire corpse is laid out on the ground and given to vultures to consume the flesh. When only the bones remain, these are broken down, mixed with barley flower and yak butter, and fed to crows.

Six Rs of healthy grief: A grief theory from Therese Rando, she recommends that in order to process grief one should (1) Recognize the loss, (2) React to the loss, (3) Recollect and Re-Experience the lost relationship, (4) Relinquish, and put the loss behind you, (5) Readjust, and (6) Reinvest.

shroud: A covering for a corpse in preparation for burial, usually in an undyed color such as white or cream.

Social Network Site memorials: Spontaneous memorials that emerge on social networks, usually in the feed of friends and family of the deceased.

spirit money: In Chinese religion, paper money printed for use in the spirit world and used to buy things in the afterlife.

Suni: The largest branch of Islam, consisting of 85–90% of Muslim adherents.

tachrichim: (Hebrew) In Judaism, the name given to the white burial shroud made of linen or muslin.

taharah: (Hebrew) In Judaism, the traditional act of washing and purifying the body, generally performed by a person trained in the traditional Jewish purification rituals.

tallit: (Hebrew) A traditional fringed shawl that is usually used by Jewish men during prayer.

tasks of mourning: Developed by JW Worden, this grief model identified four primary tasks: (1) Accept the reality of the loss, (2) experience the pain of grief, (3) adjust to an environment without the deceased, and (4) re-invest in other relationships.

terminal lucidity: The term for the brief and often unexpected return of lucidity and consciousness right before death.

thanatology: The study of death and dying.

Theravada: One of the three schools of Buddhism, Theravada is a primarily monastic sect found in Thailand, Cambodia, Sri Lanka, and Burma centered on the arhat ideal, or self-enlightenment.

towers of silence: (dakhma; Parsi) Zoroastrian funeral tower built of stone usually placed on a hill for the disposal of the dead through excarnation. The towers were usually twenty-five meters in height, and on the inside had grates that corpses were laid on to allow for easy exposure to both the elements and vultures. The sides of the tower were higher than the middle so that people could not see the bodies as they were consumed by vultures.

transhumanism: The idea that technology and scientific advancement can be used to circumvent human limitations such as sickness, suffering, and death itself.

'uhane: (Hawai'ian) In Hawai'ian religion, the soul or spirit of a deceased person.

urns: Containers specifically made to hold cremains, or ashes of the dead.

uwe helu: (Hawai'ian) A funeral lament, meant to both welcome the dead and to honor their life.

Vajrayana: One of the three schools of Buddhism centered on esoteric rituals and found in both Tibet and the Shingon sect in Japan.

vand chakna: (Punjabi) Literally translated as giving one's earnings to others, this is the third duty of being a Sikh, and means that one should give to charity and care for others.

viduy: In Judaism, a prayer of confession generally recited before death.

Waheguru: (Punjabi) The Sikh name for God, and literally translated as wonderful teacher.

whole brain death: Death defined as the irreversible loss of function of the higher brain and the brainstem, which can often be indicated by a permanent loss of consciousness and the loss of a patient's ability to breathe on one's own.

will: A legally binding government document that explains what to do with one's possessions and estate once one has died.

yahrzeit: (Hebrew) In Judaism, the celebration of the anniversary of a death.

yawm al-din: (Arabic; day of judgment; sometimes also romanized as yawm ad-din) In Islam, this term describes the judgment day that Muslims believe occurs when one dies, and determines whether one goes to heaven or to hell.

yizkor: In Judaism, a special memorial prayer that is prayed four times a year for the deceased.

zombie: A corpse said to be revived from the dead.

INDEX

abhishekam: 45, 148

advanced directive: 2–3, 26, 30, 148

African American: 54, 95, 120, 124; abuse of by medical system 18; deathways 24, 25; morbidity rates 20–21; perspectives on good death 18–19

afterlife: x, xiv, xv, xvii, xvii, 1, 4, 18, 40, 42, 44, 51, 59, 83, 98, 100, 123, 138, 139, 140, 146, 155, 161; in Buddhism 90, 109–111; in Chinese religions 48, 49, 57, 91–93, 111–112; in Christianity 51, 52, 58, 113–120; corrupted 145; in Hinduism 106–108; in Islam 6, 55, 104–106; in indigenous traditions 20, 96, 97, 120–121; in Judaism 43, 100; in Sikhism 108; in secular culture 61; technological 67, 126, 137

'aha'aina waimaka: 122, 148

akhirah: 104, 148

alkaline hydrolysis: see resomation

All Souls' Day: 113–116, 148

'amakua: 120, 149

antam sanskaar: 47, 149

aquamation: see resomation

aquiline hydrolysis: see resomation

Ariès, Phillippe: xi, 70, 80

atman: 106, 149

augmented reality (AR): 126

autopsy: 44

avatar: 128, 136–139, 152

baptism: 16, 104, 149

Baptist: 17

barsi: 109, 149

barzakh: 105, 149

Becker, Ernst: 70, 80

Before Your Eyes: 138

bereavement: xvi, 70, 77, 80, 87, 95, 119, 126, 128, 132, 134, 137, 146; definition of 71, 149; leave 71–72, 149; purpose of 72–73

bodhisattvas: 11, 149

body: 3, 4, 9, 10, 12, 13, 19, 20, 21, 27, 28, 30, 31, 34, 35, 52, 54, 56, 59, 60, 62, 64, 65, 67, 78, 87, 88–91, 93, 96, 97, 105, 106, 111, 113, 117, 119, 120–122, 145, 146, 148, 149, 159, 161, 162; disposal of 26, 40, 150, 151, 152; embalming of 41, 48, 51, 153; farms 65–66; polluting effects of 47, 48; washing of 5, 18, 42–47, 49, 50, 55, 91, 148, 162

Bon Odori: 111, 150

brain death: see death

Buddha: 11, 13, 90

Buddhism: attitude towards animal death in 21; comparison to Hinduism 45–46; core teachings of 11–13; cremation in 60; mourning traditions in 89–90; preparation of the body in 47–48; rejection of embalmment by 42; remembrance rituals in 110–111; Tibetan 62; views of afterlife in 109–110

burial: xv, 3, 4, 21, 40, 41, 43–51, 54, 56–62, 84, 85, 90, 96–98, 101, 105, 106, 112, 114, 119, 151, 155, 160; green 65, 154; natural 65, 158; reef 61, 132; shroud 43, 55, 161, 162; sky 62, 161; vault liners 65, 150

cardio-pulmonary death: *see* death

care: xvii, 10, 13, 26, 32, 48, 78, 83, 85, 87, 92, 93, 95, 98, 105, 107, 110, 111, 112, 113, 120, 131, 144, 148, 156, 157, 163; curative 29, 151; death 41, 42, 52; end-of-life xii, 14, 16, 17, 18, 31, 153; hospice 29, 154; medical xii, xv, 12, 37, 153, 154, 159; palliative xiii, 5, 8, 9, 13, 29–30, 146, 152, 155, 159

casket: 52–56, 58–59, 65, 150

Catholic: *see* Roman Catholic

celebration of life: 63, 95, 150

cemetery: xi, 50, 53, 55, 56, 86, 97, 102, 116, 161; visitation 105, 117

chaplain: 2, 16, 30, 146

Cherokee: 151, afterlife beliefs of 121; burial practices 50, 97; mourning traditions 96; Nation Remembrance Day 122, 150; remembrance traditions 122

China: 11, 12, 14, 57, 60, 70, 88, 90, 91, 111, 131, 144, 157, 160

Chinese religion: afterlife beliefs in 111–112; disposal in 57, 60, 61, 131; ghost stories in 144; mourning traditions in 91–93; perception of death and dying 14–15; preparation of the body 48–49; remembrance rituals 112–113; san jiao 13

Chptr: 136

chrismation: 16, 150

Christianity: 7, 104, 149, 150, 152, 154; afterlife beliefs of 109; Evangelical 17, 52, 118; imagined embodiment in 50–52; mind/body dualism in 146; Orthodox: *see* Orthodox Christianity; Protestant: *see* Protestantism; Roman Catholic: *see* Roman Catholicism; understandings of death and dying 15–19

coffin: 49, 52 54, 55, 59, 60, 150

columbarium: 57, 61, 151

composting: 59, 64–65, 150

condolence: 90, 106

confirmation: 16, 151

Confucianism: 13, 151

Continuing Bonds Theory: 75–76, 134, 137, 151

corpse: 4, 31, 49, 52, 90, 145, 153, 163; disposal of 59, 61, 62, 64, 65, 151, 153, 160, 161, 162; incorrupt 51, 155; preparation of 40, 49, 91; preservation of 40–42, 48, 51; public display of 41, 48

COVID-19: 127

cremains: 60–61, 64, 96, 151

cremation: 40, 46, 48, 50, 57, 59–61, 63, 64, 67, 88–90, 96, 117, 119, 151

cryonics: 61, 66–67, 68, 151

dakhma: 62, 151, 162

Daoism: 13, 151, 160

dead clothes: 96, 151

death: animal 21–22; brain 34–36, 121, 150, 159, 163; cardio-pulmonary 31–34, 150; confessions at time of 104, 151; definition of xv, 4, 31, 32, 34–37, 146, 151; education xiii, plans 2, 3; "good" 2, 5, 6, 7, 8, 10, 11, 13–22, 26, 31,

94, 146, 154; study of: xvii, x, xi, xii, xv, 2, 26, 70, 162
dharma: 13, 152
Día de los Muertos: 115–117, 152, 159
Dickinson, George: xii, xvii
Discord: 128, 132
Disposal: xiv, xv, xvi, 2, 20, 21, 26, 37, 40–69, 96, 126, 146
disposition: *see* disposal
DSM-5: 77
dual-process model: 75, 152
dying: xi, xii, xiv, 1, 2, 3, 4, 5, 6, 7, 8, 9, 11, 12, 14, 17, 18, 19, 20, 21, 22, 27, 37, 43, 52, 71, 73, 83, 94, 100, 104, 126, 138, 139, 151, 152, 162; active 28, 148; early stages of 27; late stages of 28; middle stages of 27–28; person 2, 3, 4, 6, 9, 17, 21, 26, 27, 28, 30, 73, 152; process xiii, xiv, 2, 5, 8, 13, 14, 20, 21, 26, 27, 29, 31, 46, 73, 146, 148; well, 26–27, 146

Eightfold path: 12, 152
embalmment: 20, 51, 52, 59; definition of 153; history of 40–42; rejection of 42, 44, 46, 55
end-of-life decisions: x, 153
eucharist: 16, 152
Europe: 15, 29, 50, 60, 76, 115, 116
euthanasia: in animals 21; in Buddhism 12; in Islam 44; in Judaism 3, 5; machines 127; in Sikhism 10
excarnation: 47, 61–62, 153
extreme unction: *see* last rites

Facebook: 127, 128, 132, 133, 134
feast: in Catholicism 116–117; in Chinese culture, 57, 91–92; in Hawai'ian culture 96, 122, 148; in Hinduism 88, 161; hospitality exchanges 79; potlatch 122–123
filial piety: 112, 153
five K's: 10, 153, 156

Four Noble Truths: 12, 153
Frankenstein: 145
Freud, Sigmund: 73, 80, 81
funeral: 13, 26, 41, 43, 44, 46, 47, 48, 50, 52, 57, 63, 65, 72, 84, 86, 87, 88, 89, 90, 92, 93, 94, 95, 96, 114, 122, 149, 153, 162; director 58; feasts 79, 86, 91, 92, 96, 122, 123, 157, 161; home xi, 4, 40, 63, 153; industry xiii, 53, 59, 128, 129, 130, 131, 135, 137; selfie 133; service 16, 40, 41, 118, 149, 150

game: 138–139
ghosts: 58, 111, 121, 144, 145, 147, 154
Gin Salat: 111, 154
Gorer, Geoffrey: xi, xvii, 70, 80
grave: African American Protestant traditions 120; in Catholicism 115, 116, 148; in Chinese religion 58, 111, 131–132, 159; in Cherokee traditions 121; funeral at 87; in Inuit traditions 97–98; in Islam 45, 56–57, 105; in Judaism 4, 102
graveyard: 61, 102, 116, 145, 151, 152
grief: xi, xiv, xiv, xvi, 52, 83, 84, 88, 91, 103, 120, 123, 126, 140, 146, 147; anticipatory 71, 149; communal 150; complicated 73; definition of 71, 154; difference from mourning 72; dual process model of 75, 152; history of the study of 70–71; integrated 105, 155; medicalized model of 77; online 127, 133, 134, 136, 138, 139; process of 70; purpose of 72–72; psychological study of 70–71; sociological study of 78–80; stage-based models of 73–74; theories of 73–77, 154, 158, 161, 162; work 73–74
gui: 111, 154
Gurmantar Waheguru: 47, 154
gurudwara: 47, 89, 154

halal: 21, 87, 154

Hawai'ian tradition: 20, 154, 155, 156, 157; afterlife beliefs 120–121, 149, 162; disposal customs 49–50; mourning traditions 96, 162; remembrance traditions 122, 148

health: x, xi, xii, 16, 20, 36

healthcare: x, xii, xiii, 5, 7, 9, 12, 14, 37, 152, 155, 157

Hinduism: 90; afterlife beliefs 106–107; attitudes towards death and dying 7–9, 159; beliefs of 7–8, 149, 158, 160; disposal 42, 60, 148; mourning customs 88; preparation of the body 45–46; remembrance traditions 107–108, 159, 161

holy orders: 16, 154

Hong Kong: 14, 61, 132

ho'oponopono: 122, 154

hospice: care xiii, 26, 29–30, 154; eligibility 29, 155; movement xi, xiii, 6, 155; pediatric xiii

hospital: xv, 6, 7, 26, 30, 31, 148; chaplains 16–17; death in xii, 6, 29, 32, 33, 46; palliative care in 29, 155

huaka'i pō: 121, 155

hun: 111, 155

icon: 58, 59, 79, 117, 155, 158

iluraijuaqtut: 98, 155

India: 7–9, 11, 22, 24, 45–47, 60, 66

indigenous: 115, 123; beliefs of afterlife 120–121; disposal traditions 49–50; mourning traditions 96–98; perceptions of death and dying 25, 44; peoples19–21; remembrance rituals 122–123

inhumation: 60, 155

Instagram: 128, 132, 133

Internet: 53, 114, 127, 131, 136; memorials on 129, 132

intiqal: 6, 155

Inuit: 20; afterlife beliefs 120, 121; disposal practices 50; mourning traditions 96, 97, 155; remembrance traditions 122

Iran: 62

Islam: 7, 47, 154, 161, 162; afterlife views in 104–105, 148, 149, 155, 16; beliefs of 5–7, 160; disposal traditions 42; dying 9; mourning traditions 86–87; perceptions of death and dying 5–6; preparation of the body 44–45; remembrance rituals 105–106

Jahannam: 104, 155

Jannah: 104, 155

Japan: 11, 12, 13, 53, 60, 76, 90, 111, 127, 144

Jesus Christ: 15, 156

Judaism: 156, 158, 161, 161; afterlife views in 43–44, 100–101, 160; beliefs of 3–4, 87, 104; disposal traditions 42, 44, 45; mourning traditions 55, 84–86; perceptions of death and dying 4–5; preparation of the body 42–43, 44; remembrance rituals 101–103, 163

judgement: in Christianity 94–95 117; in Islam 104–105; ten courts of judgement 111

kaccha: 10, 153, 156

kaddish: 101–102, 156

kanga: 10, 153, 156

kapu: 121, 156

kara: 10, 153, 156

karhah prashad: 89, 156

karma: 7, 8, 11, 12, 106, 107, 108, 109, 156, 160

Kastenbaum, Robert: xii, xiii

Keen, Sam: 143

keriah: 86, 156

kesh: 10, 153, 156

kirpan: 10, 153, 156

kirt karna: 9, 156

kirtan sohila: 89, 157

Klass, Dennis: 75, 76, 80, 81, 134, 141, 151
koliva: 59, 118, 157
Korea: 11, 13, 90, 139
kosher: 21, 22, 87
Kübler-Ross, Elisabeth: xiii, xvii, 73, 74, 80

Lady of the Dead: 115, 116, 157
last rites: 17
life expectancy: 12, 36–37, 70, 157
Lindeman, Erich: 74, 80
living will: 3, 26, 30, 48, 148
loss orientation: 75, 152, 157

Mahayana: 11, 89, 149, 157
makaria: 94, 157
mana: 50, 120, 157
mass casualty: 79, 157
masses for the dead: 95, 113–114, 115, 117, 157
medical culture: x, xv, 1, 2, 6
medical school: xii, 35
medical system: 1, 16, 18, 29, 31, 36, 77
medicine: x, xi, xiii, xv, 1, 3, 5, 6, 18, 32, 36, 78, 145
memorial: 46, 60, 61, 63, 88, 95, 102, 103, 105, 110, 118, 119, 123, 139, 144, 157, 158, 163; digital 127–129, 152; funeral industry driven sites 129–131; 153; Online Support Network (OSN) 128, 135, 137, 159; smartphone 135–136; Social Network Sites (SNS) 128, 132–134, 137, 161; virtual 131–132, 138, 140
memorialization: 62, 79, 88, 100, 119, 127, 128, 129, 131, 132, 135, 136, 138, 144, 157
memory drawer: 58, 158
Mexico: 115–117, 152
Mictecacihuatl: 115, 157
minyan: 86, 158, 161
Mitford, Jessica: xiii, xviii, 69
mizuko kuyō: 144, 147
moksha: 8, 158

monster: 144–146
morbidity: 4
mortality: 94, 138; rates 19, 36–37, 70, 158
mourning: xiv, 51, 70, 73, 100, 146, 150, 151; definition of 72, 158; difference from bereavement 71–72; difference from grief 79; digital 126, 128, 130, 132–137; excessive 45; in Buddhism 89–90; in Chinese religions 91–93; in Christianity 93–95, 119, 120; in Hinduism 88; in Islam 86–87, 105; in Judaism 3, 84–86, 101, 156 161; in indigenous traditions 96–98, 121, 122, 148,155; public 70; purpose of 72; religious 83; in Sikhism 47, 88–89, 108–109; tasks of 74–75, 162
mukti: 10, 158
Mul mantar: 47, 158
Muslim: 5, 6, 6, 23, 44, 45, 54, 55, 56, 57, 86, 87, 104, 105, 106, 109, 113, 161, 162, 163

nam japna: 9, 158
Narrative Grief Therapy: 75–76, 158
Native American: afterlife beliefs 120–121; disposal customs 49–50; mourning traditions 96–98; remembrance rituals 122–123; view of death 19–21
Neimeyer, Robert: 76, 80, 158
Nickman, Steven L.: 75, 76, 80, 134, 141, 151
nightmarchers: 121
nirvana: 11, 109, 159

organ donation: 3, 10, 18, 20, 31, 34, 35, 45, 47, 119, 146, 159
Orthodox Christianity: 50, 53, 54, 150, 155, 157, 159; afterlife beliefs of 95, 113, 117; description of 15–16; disposal in 58–59; mourning traditions 94–95; remembrance rituals of 118

palliative care: xiii, 5, 8, 9, 13, 29–30, 146, 152, 155, 159

Pan de Muerto buns: 116, 159

Parnia Lab: 32, 34, 38

penance: 16, 159

phone: 92, 126, 127, 131, 132, 135, 136, 139

pictures: 9, 57, 58, 93, 116, 117, 134, 136, 153, 158, 159; posting online 130, 132, 133

Pinterest: 128, 132

pitri: 107, 159

pitru paksha: 107, 159

po: 111, 159

prayer: 64, 72; cards 114, 158, 159; of confession 4, 5, 163; in Buddhism 11, 90, 110, 127, 150; in Catholicism 17, 58, 93, 113, 114, 157; in Cherokee tradition 97; in Chinese religion 48, 49, 111, 112, 131,132, 160; in Eastern Orthodoxy 94, 95, 117, 118; in Hawai'ian tradition 96; in Hinduism 7; intercessory 114, 115, 117, 155; in Islam 6, 7, 55, 87, 105, 106; in Judaism 4, 43, 55, 85, 86, 101, 102, 103, 156, 158, 161, 162, 163; in Protestantism 17; in Sikhism 46, 47, 89, 109, 149, 157

predestination: 6, 160

promession: 64, 160

Protestantism: 74, 76, 117; beliefs of afterlife 113, 118–119; disposal traditions 52, 54, 58–59; mourning traditions 95; perceptions of death and dying 15–19; remembrance rituals 119–120

purgatory: 17, 51, 58, 94, 101, 105, 113, 115, 160

qing ming: 48, 111, 112, 131, 160

qingtuan: 112, 160

QR codes: 131, 132

Rando, Therese: 74, 80, 161

reincarnation: 7, 8, 9, 10, 20, 43, 60, 100, 106, 108, 117, 160

resomation: 59, 62, 148, 149

restoration orientation: 75, 152, 160

resurrection: 43, 94, 100, 104, 118, 119, 160

Roman Catholicism: 15, 47, 101, 115, 148, 151, 155, 159, 160; beliefs of 15–17; afterlife 51–52, 113; disposal traditions 54, 58, 60, 67; mourning traditions 93–94; perceptions of death and dying 16–17; remembrance rituals 94, 101, 110, 113–117

Russia: 15

sabbath: 84, 101, 102

Sahib, Guru Granth: 89, 154, 158

samsara: 8, 10, 11, 106, 109, 160

san jiao: 13, 160

sangha: 110, 160

Saunders, Dame Cicely: xi, xiii, xviii, 155

Schut, Henk: 75, 80, 81, 152, 160

secular: 13, 76, 112, 143, 147

secularism: 147

seudat havra'ah: 86, 161

Seventh day Adventists: 22

Shabbat: 84, 161

Shahadah: 104, 160

Shelley, Mary: 145, 147

shen: 111, 161

Sheol: 43, 160

Shi'a: 5, 161

shiva minyan: 86, 161

shiva: 84, 85, 86, 101, 156, 161

shomer: 4, 161

shraddha: 88, 107, 161

shroud: 43, 44, 45, 46, 50, 54, 55, 97, 161

sickness: xi, 3, 4, 66, 98, 104, 137, 162

Sikhism: 9, 149, 153, 154, 156, 157, 158, 163; beliefs of 10–11; afterlife 108; disposal traditions 60; mourning traditions 88–89; perceptions of death and dying 10–11; preparation of the body

46–47; remembrance rituals
108–109
Silverman, Phyllis R.: 75, 76, 80,
134, 141, 151
Singapore: 57, 60, 61, 112, 127
six R's of healthy grief: 74, 161
sky burial: 62, 161
soul: 4, 6, 10, 13, 19, 46, 47, 49, 51,
58, 84, 90, 95, 98, 101, 103, 104,
105, 106, 107, 109, 110, 111, 113,
114, 116, 117, 119, 120, 121, 122,
145, 146, 149, 155, 159, 160, 162
Southeast Asia: 11, 13, 22
spirit: 13, 19, 20, 21, 50, 55, 92, 107,
111, 115, 120, 144, 158, 159, 160,
161, 162; guardian 120, 149;
money 57, 92–93, 112; house
92–93; in tablet 91; wandering 121
Stroebe, Margaret: 75, 80, 81,
152, 162
suffering: 5, 7, 8, 12, 13, 14, 19, 27,
28, 29, 66, 71, 104, 106, 107, 137,
151, 153, 155, 162
suicide: 5, 6, 8, 10, 12, 16, 20, 21,
36, 66, 110, 127, 135, 144
Suni: 162

tachrichim: 43, 162
taharah: 42, 162
tallit: 43, 162
technologies: xiv, xv, xvi, 5, 35, 66,
126, 133, 146
terminal lucidity: 28, 162
Thailand :11, 12, 90, 111, 112,
154, 162
thanatechnologies: 137, 139, 140
thanatology: x, xi, xiv, xv, 162
That Dragon, Cancer: 138
Theravada: 11, 22, 89, 162

Tibet: 11, 22, 47, 62, 109, 161, 163
towers of silence: 62, 162
transhumanism: xvi, 66, 137,
141, 162
Twitter: 128, 132, 133, 134

'uhane: 120, 162
underworld: in Chinese religion 49,
57, 58, 92, 93, 111; in Hawai'ian
religion 120; in Inuit tradition 121
United Kingdom: xiii, 1, 39, 60, 70,
76, 155
United States: xiii, 1, 14, 15, 16, 17,
18, 20, 33, 36, 37, 39, 41, 46, 51,
53, 54, 55, 56, 60, 63, 64, 65, 66,
67, 72, 76, 77, 116, 123, 129,
131, 143
urn: 61, 162
uwe helu: 96, 162

Vajrayana: 11, 89, 163
vand chakna: 9, 163
viduy: 4, 5, 163
Vietnam: 11, 48, 112, 157
visitation: 40, 41, 44, 45, 55, 88,
130, 153

Waheguru :10, 46, 47, 88, 89, 108,
154, 163
Walter, Tony: xi, xviii, 70, 81, 82,
93, 98, 113, 124, 142
Worden, J. William :74, 75, 81, 162

yahrzeit: 102, 163
yawm al-din: 104, 163
yizkor: 102, 163

zombie: 144, 145, 147, 163
Zoroastrianism: 62

Printed in the United States
by Baker & Taylor Publisher Services